This Coloring Book Belongs To:

Color Chart

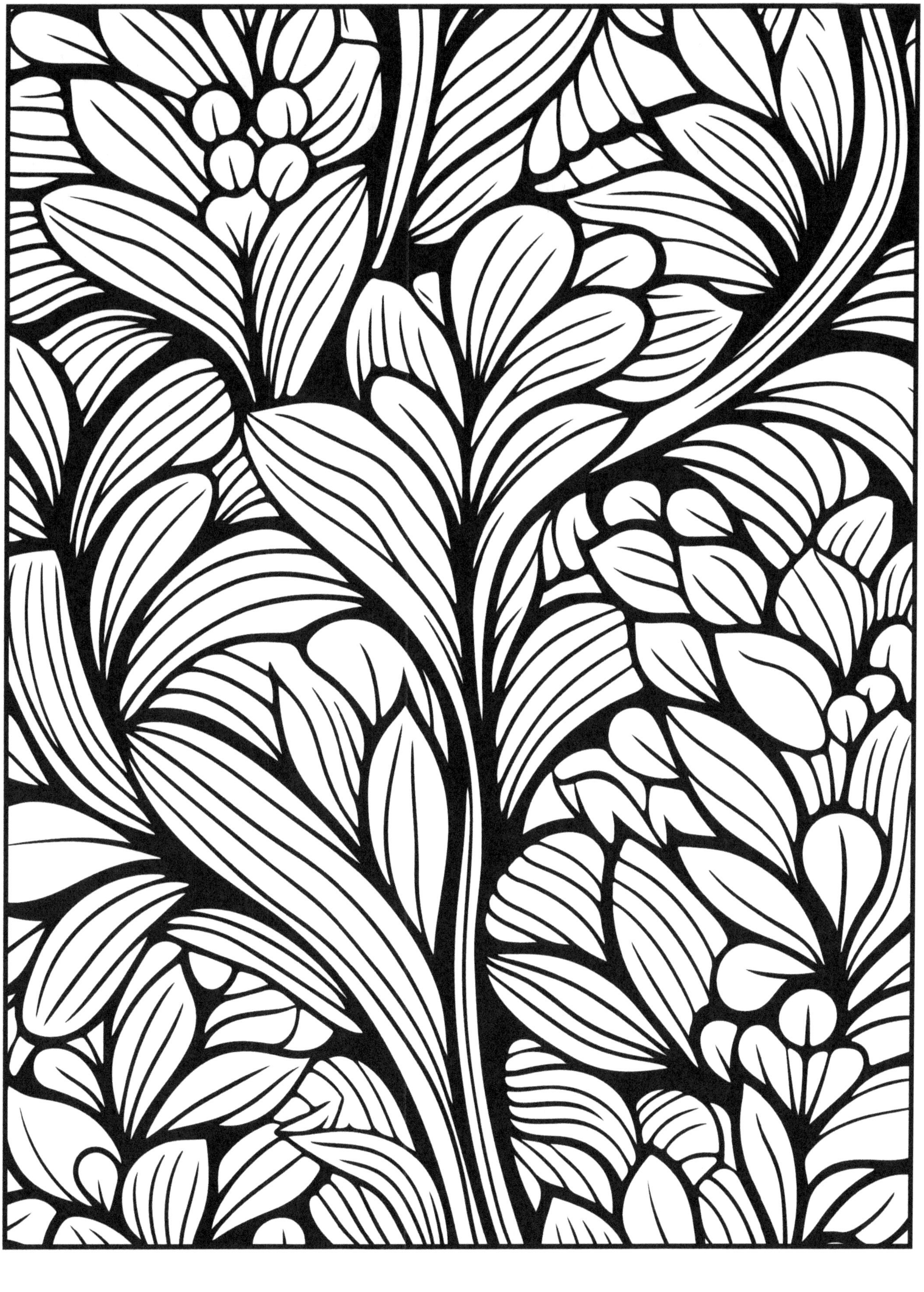

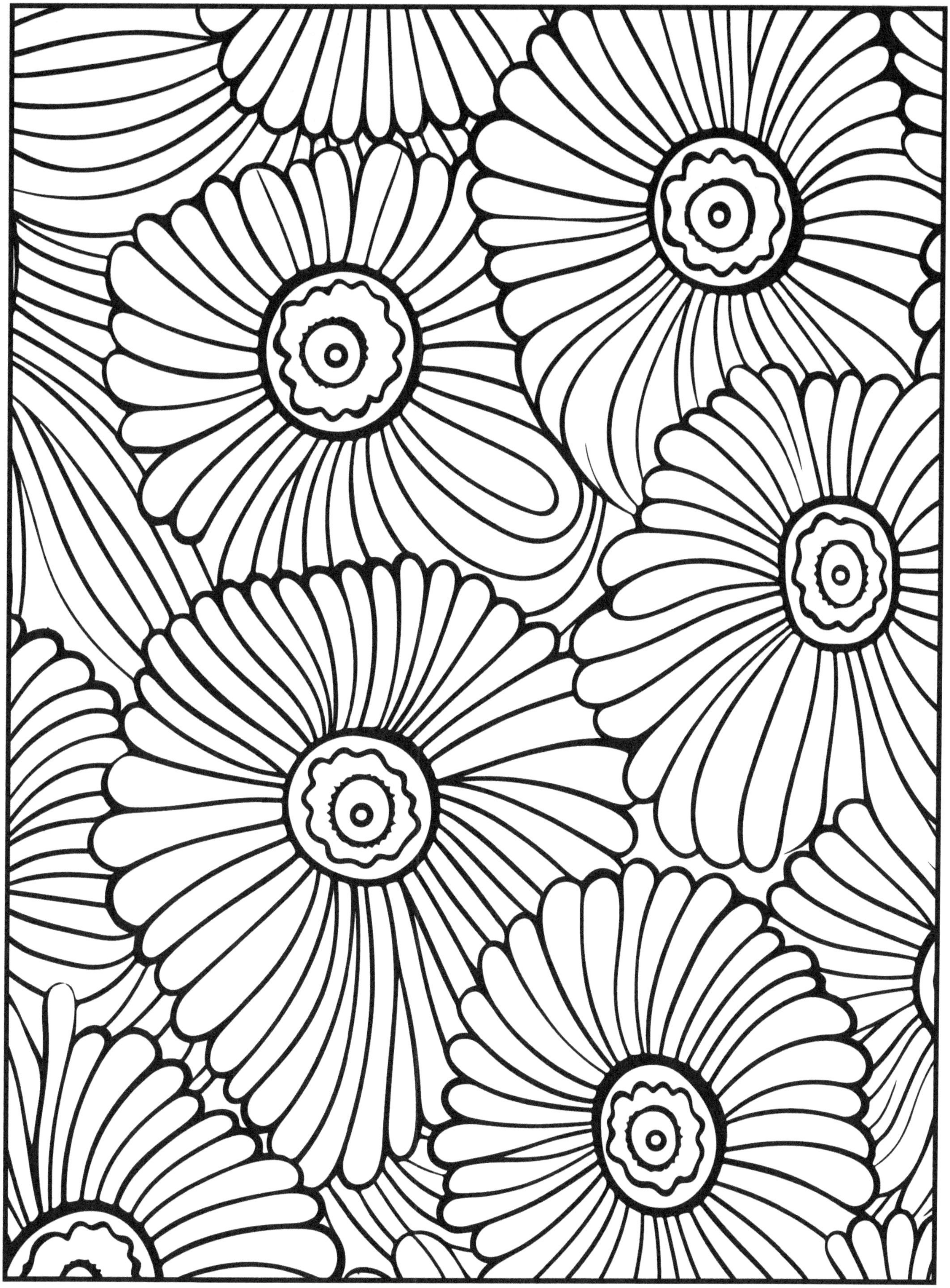

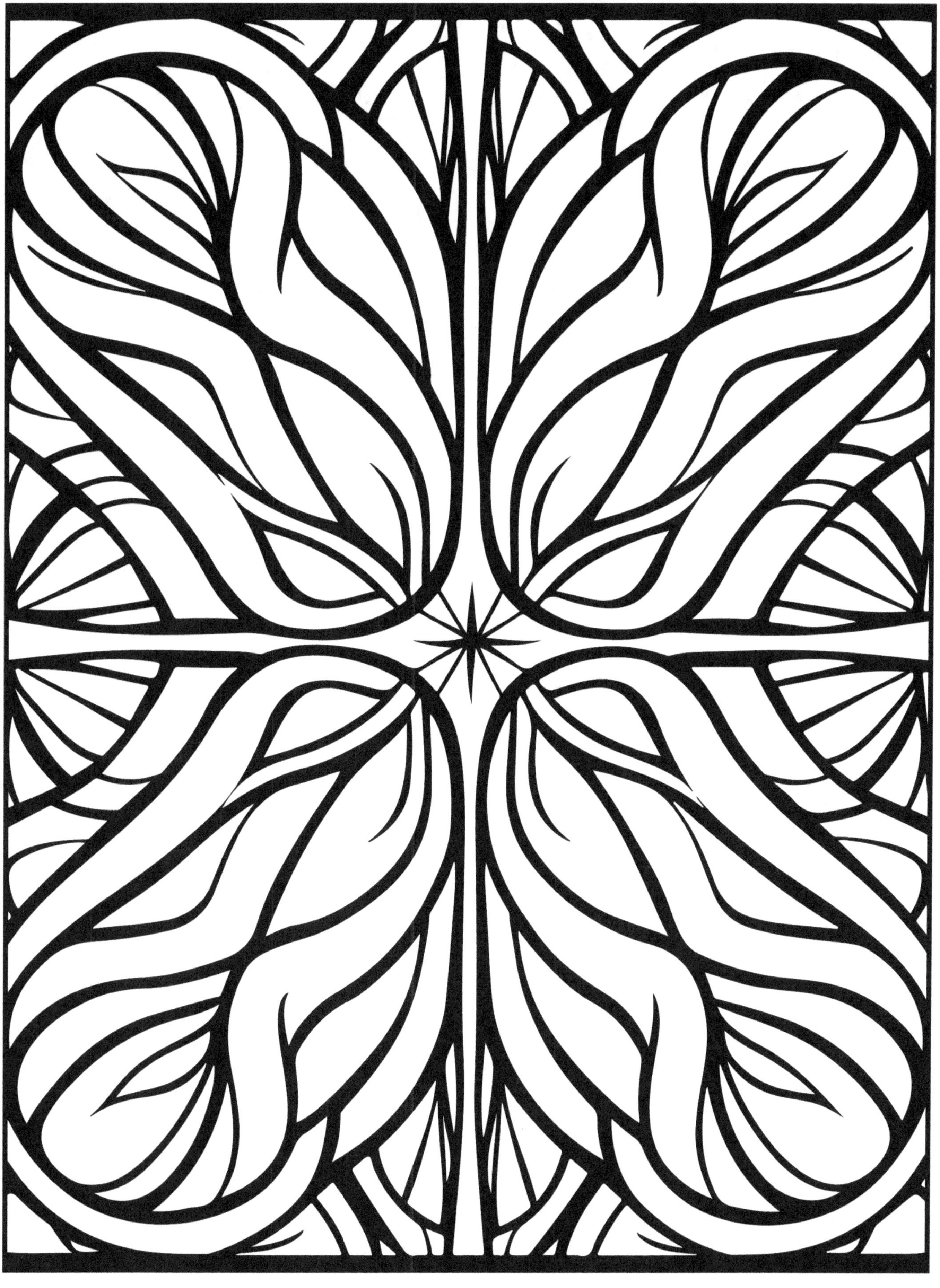

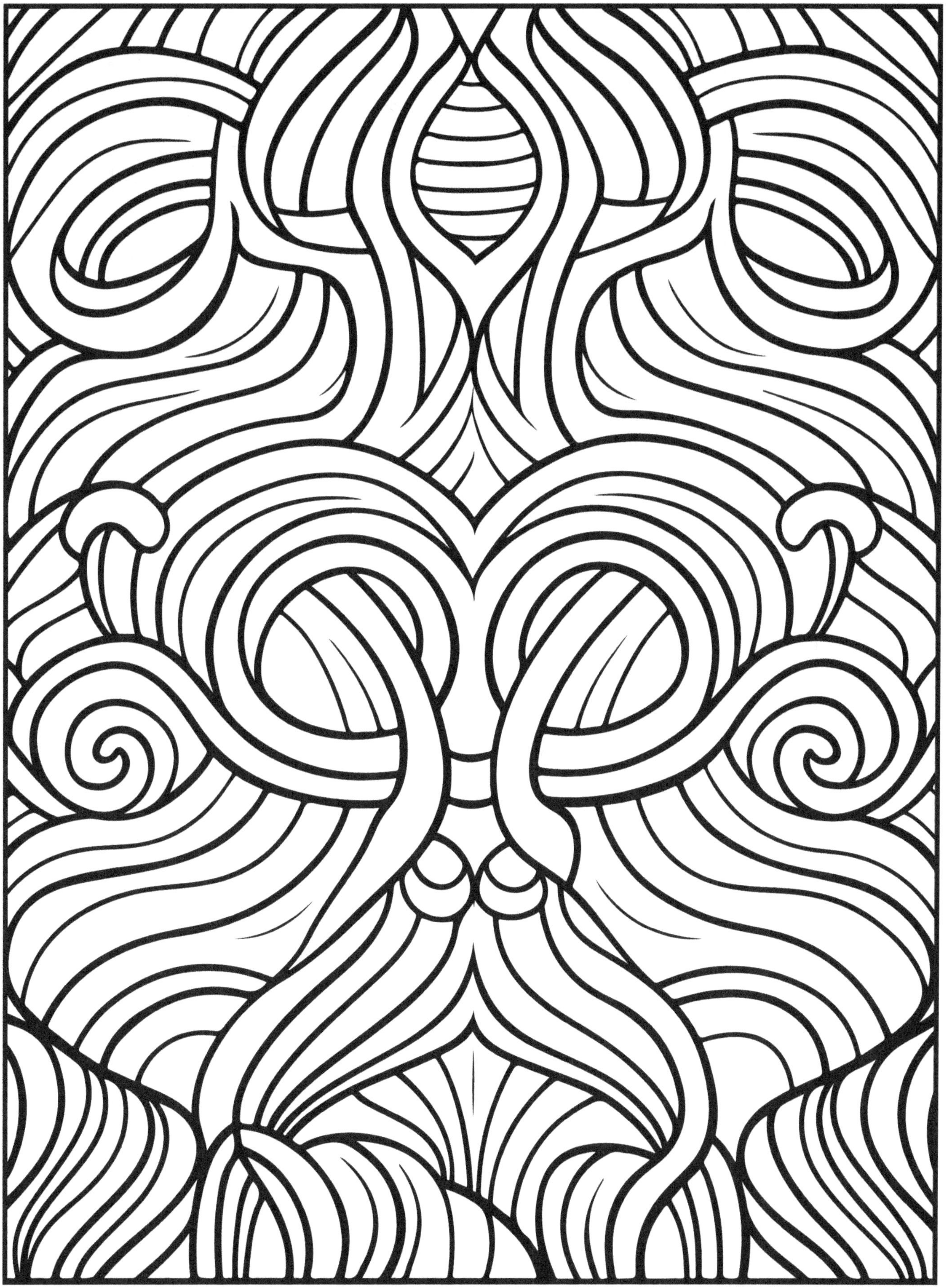

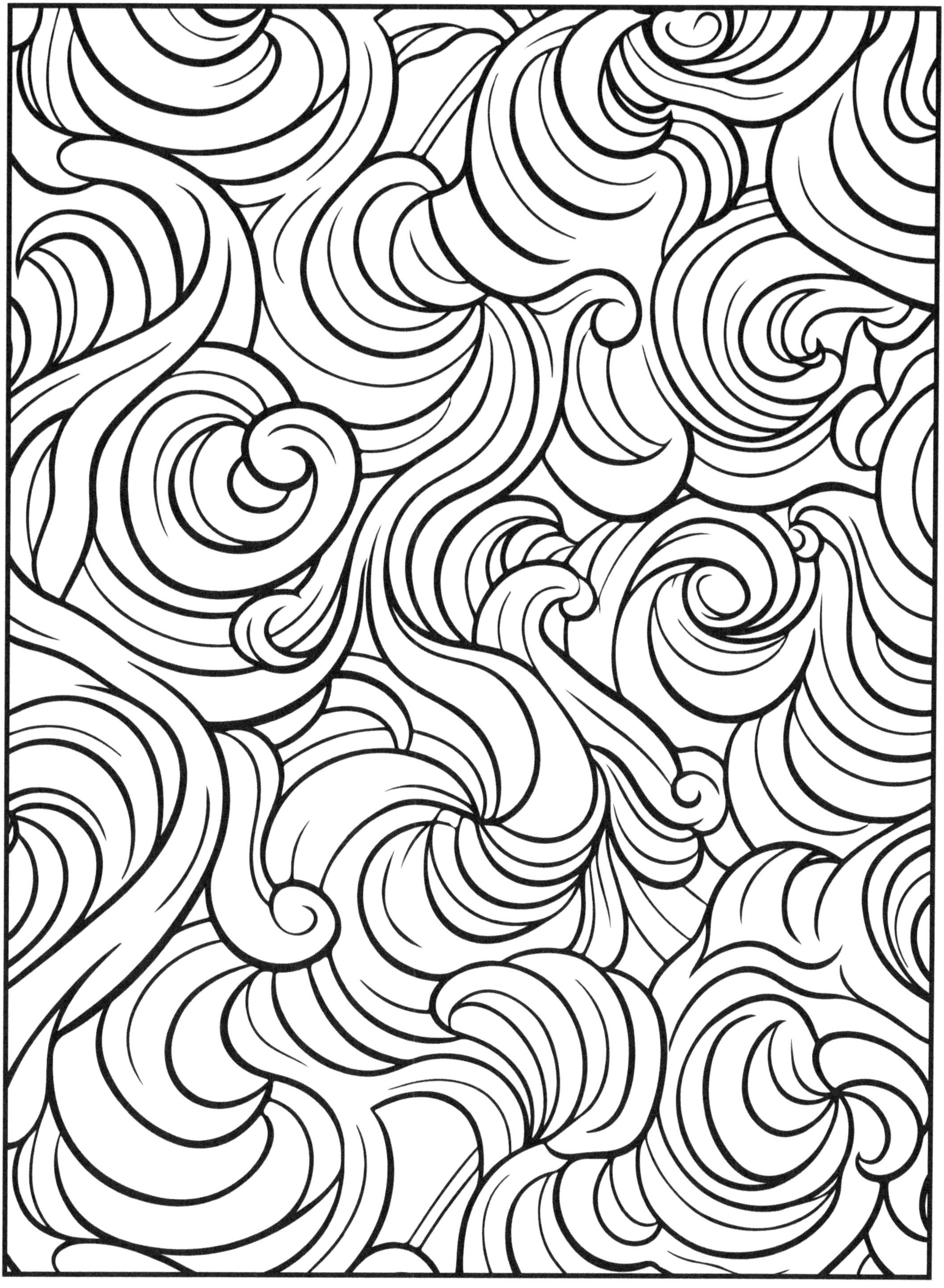

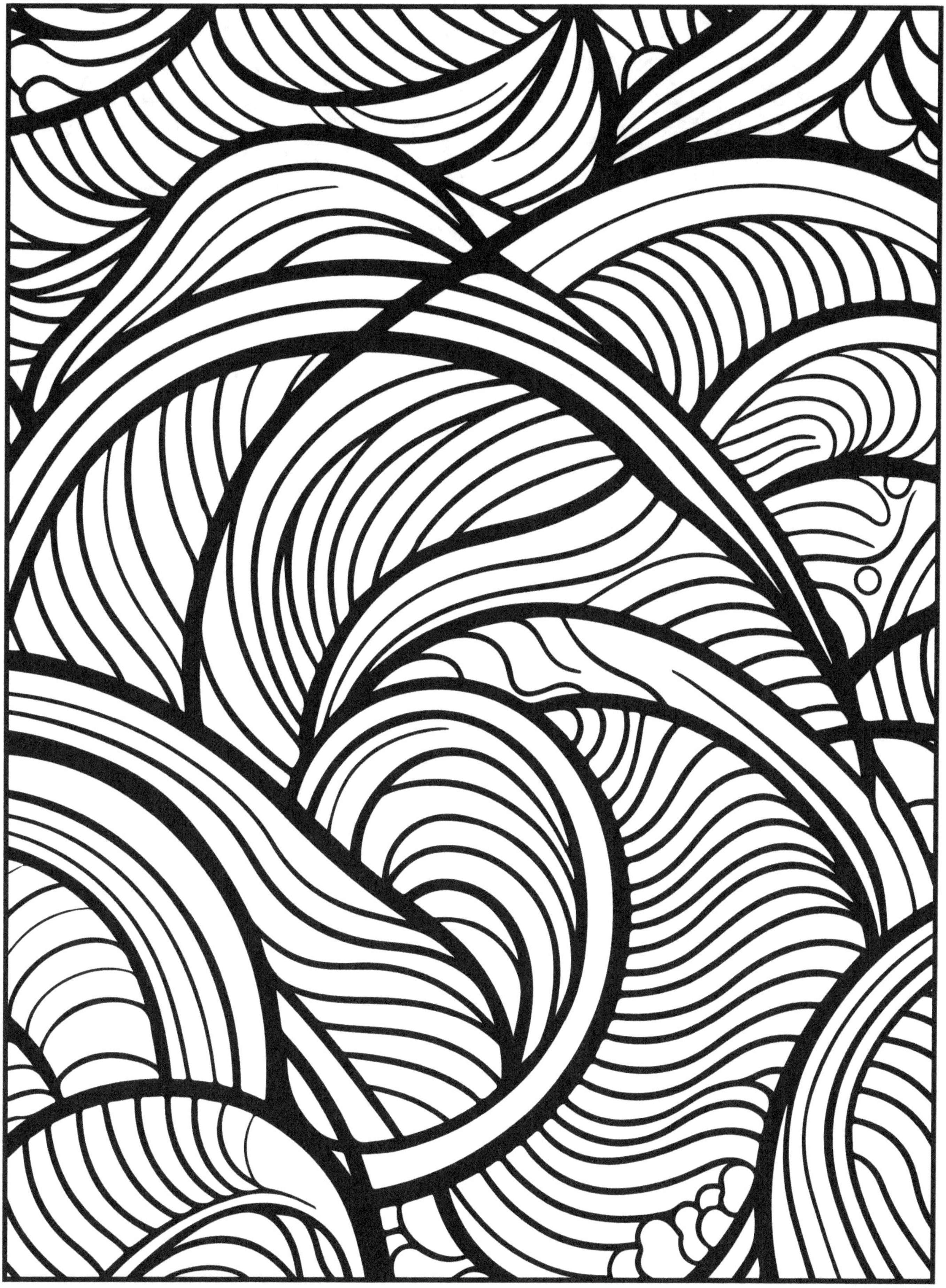

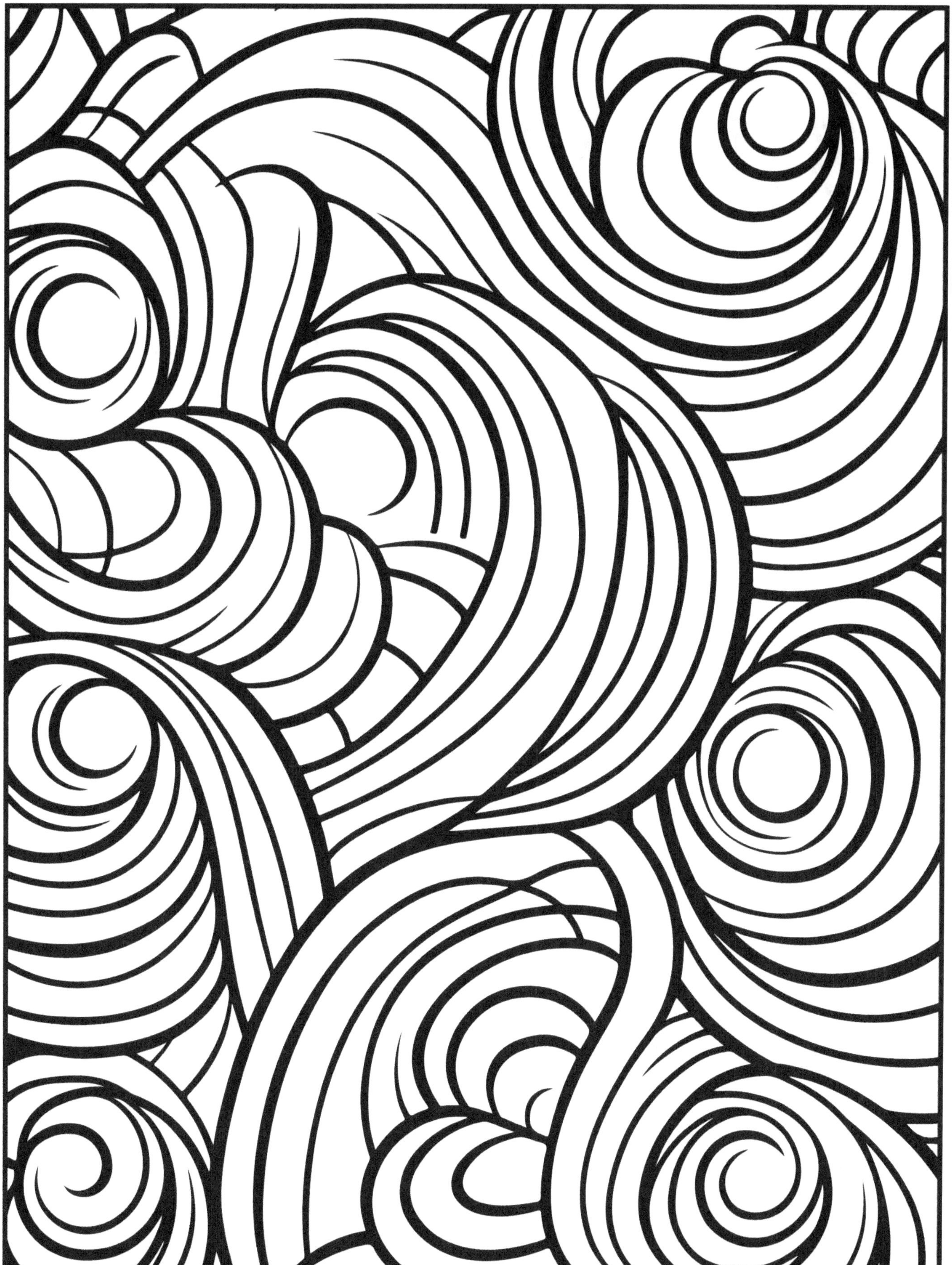

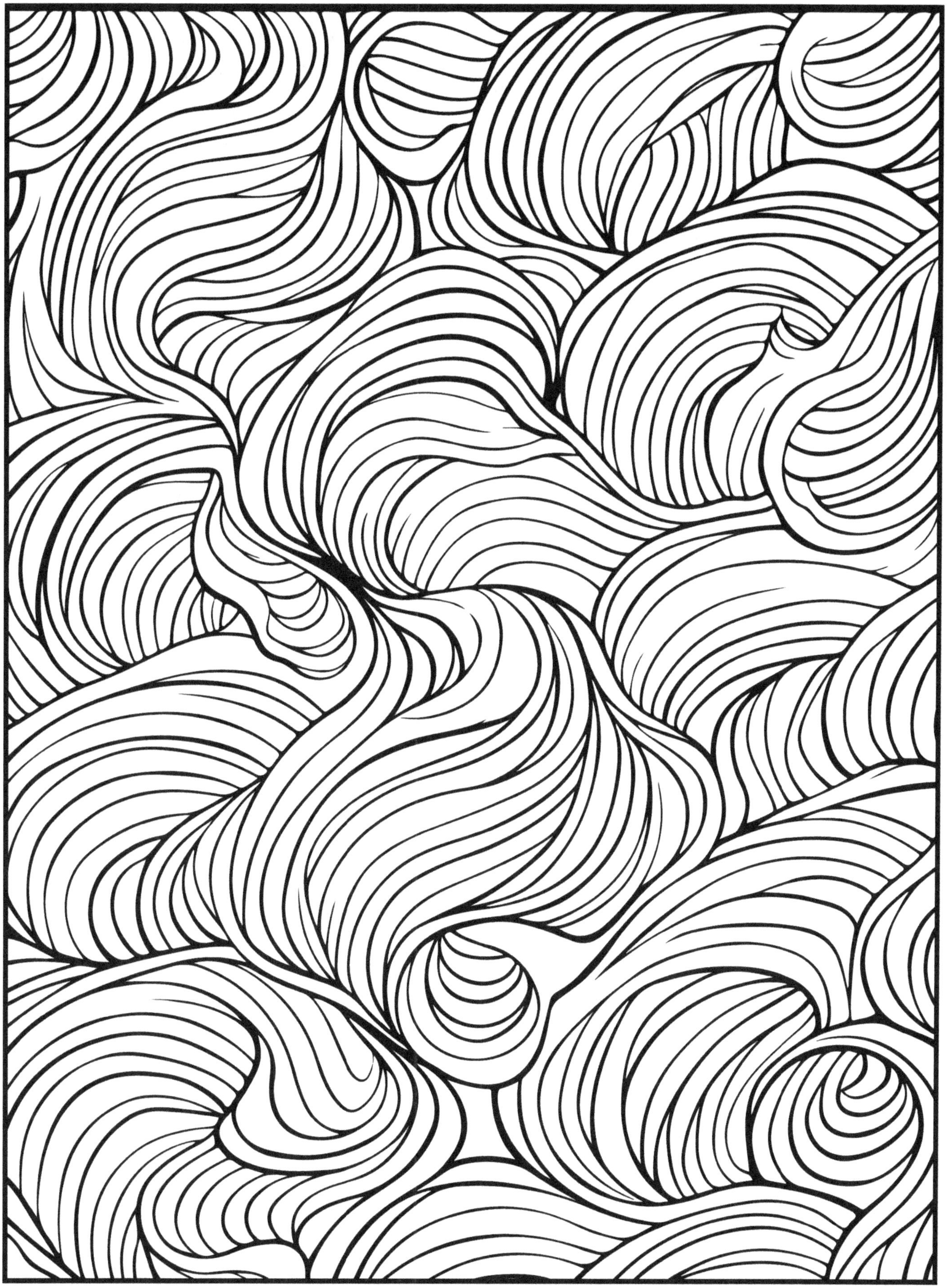

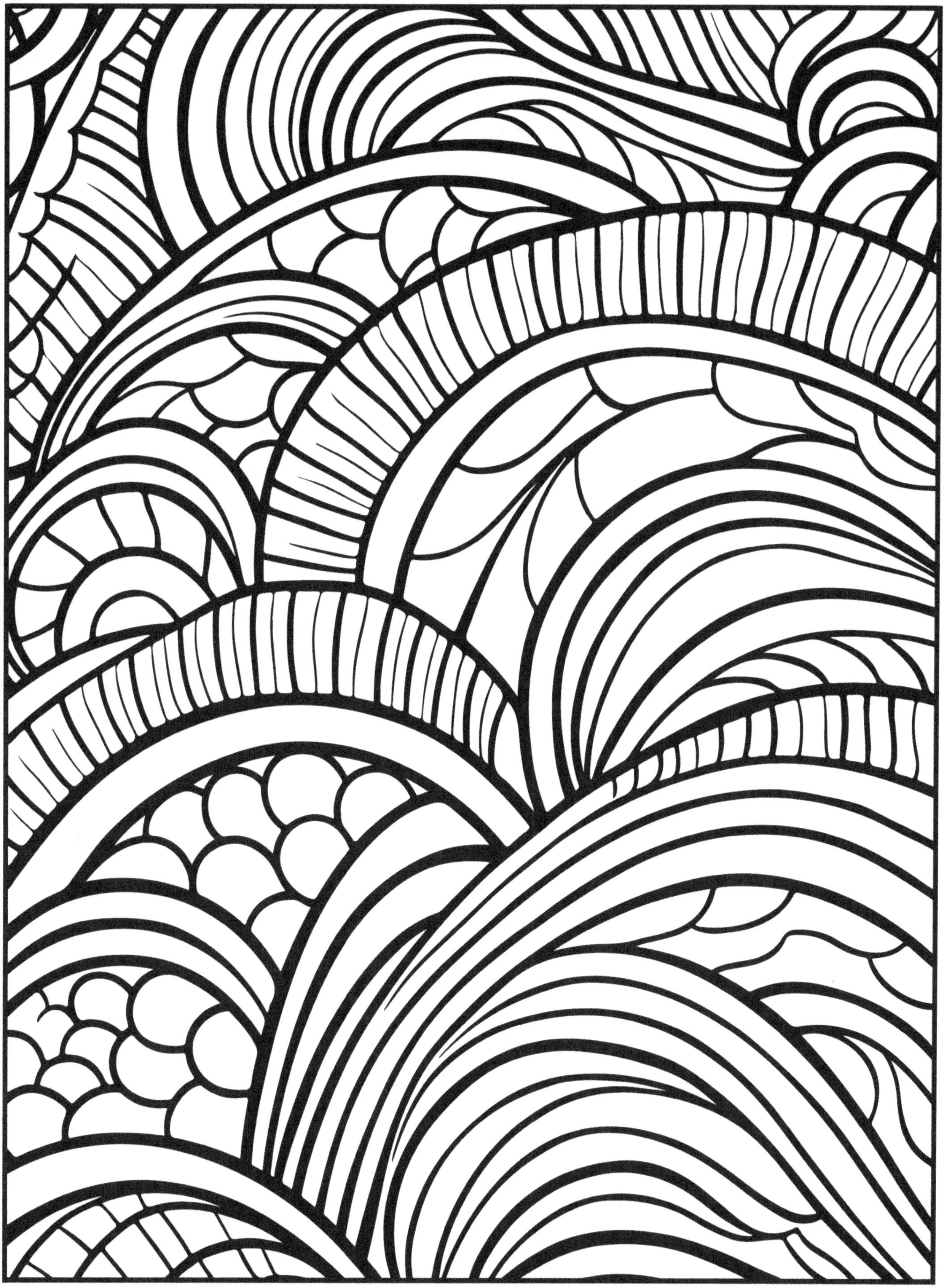

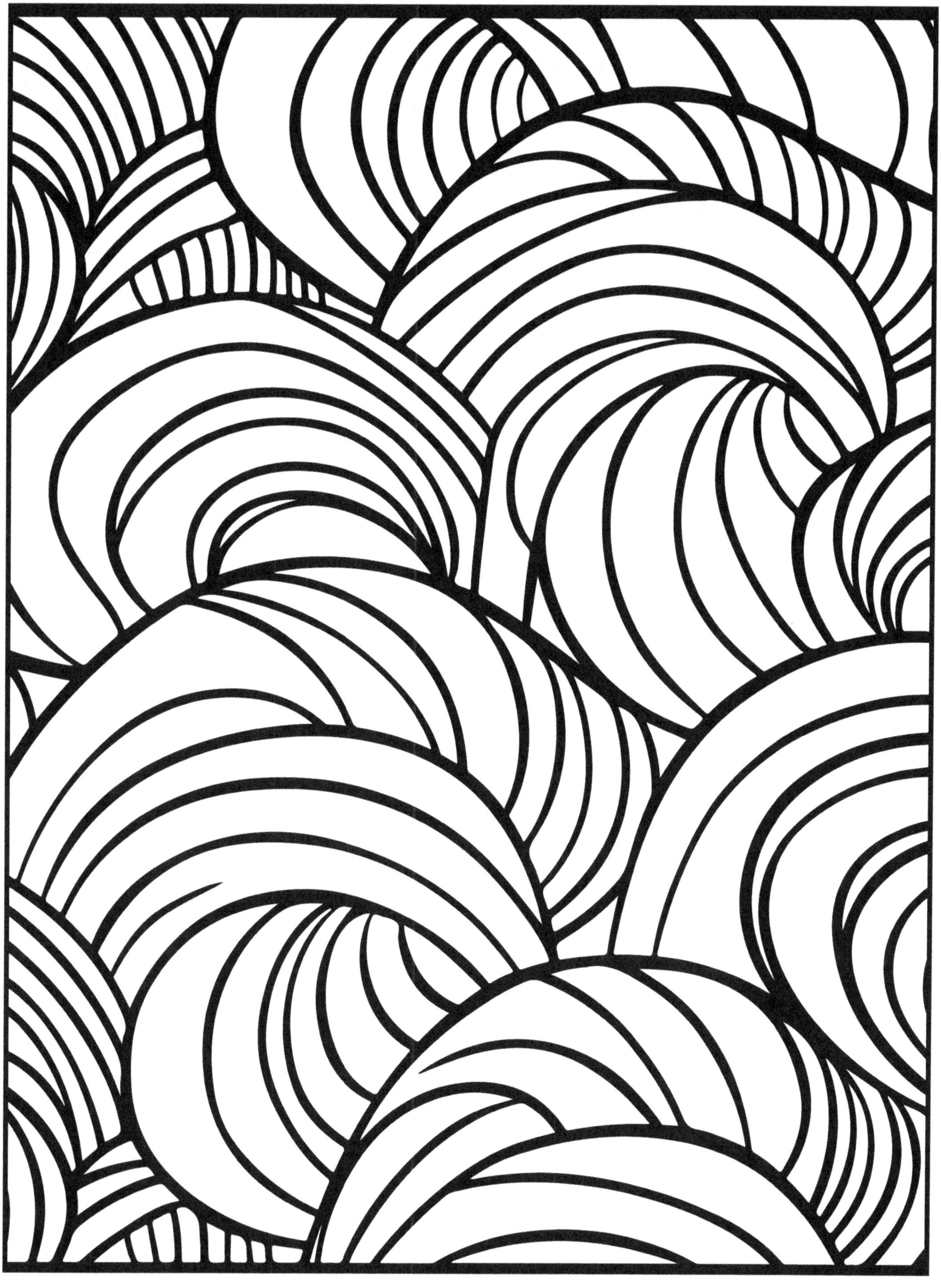

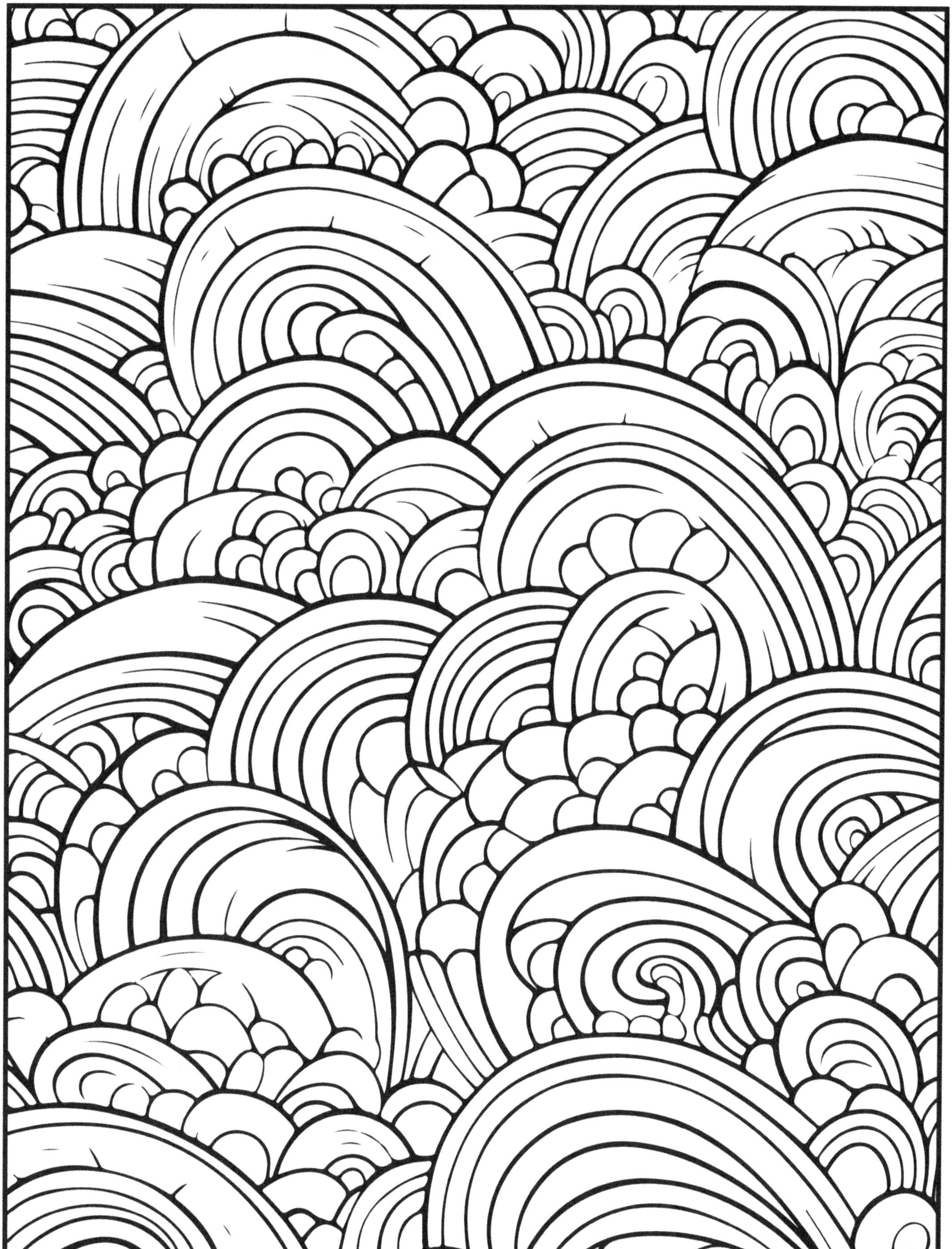

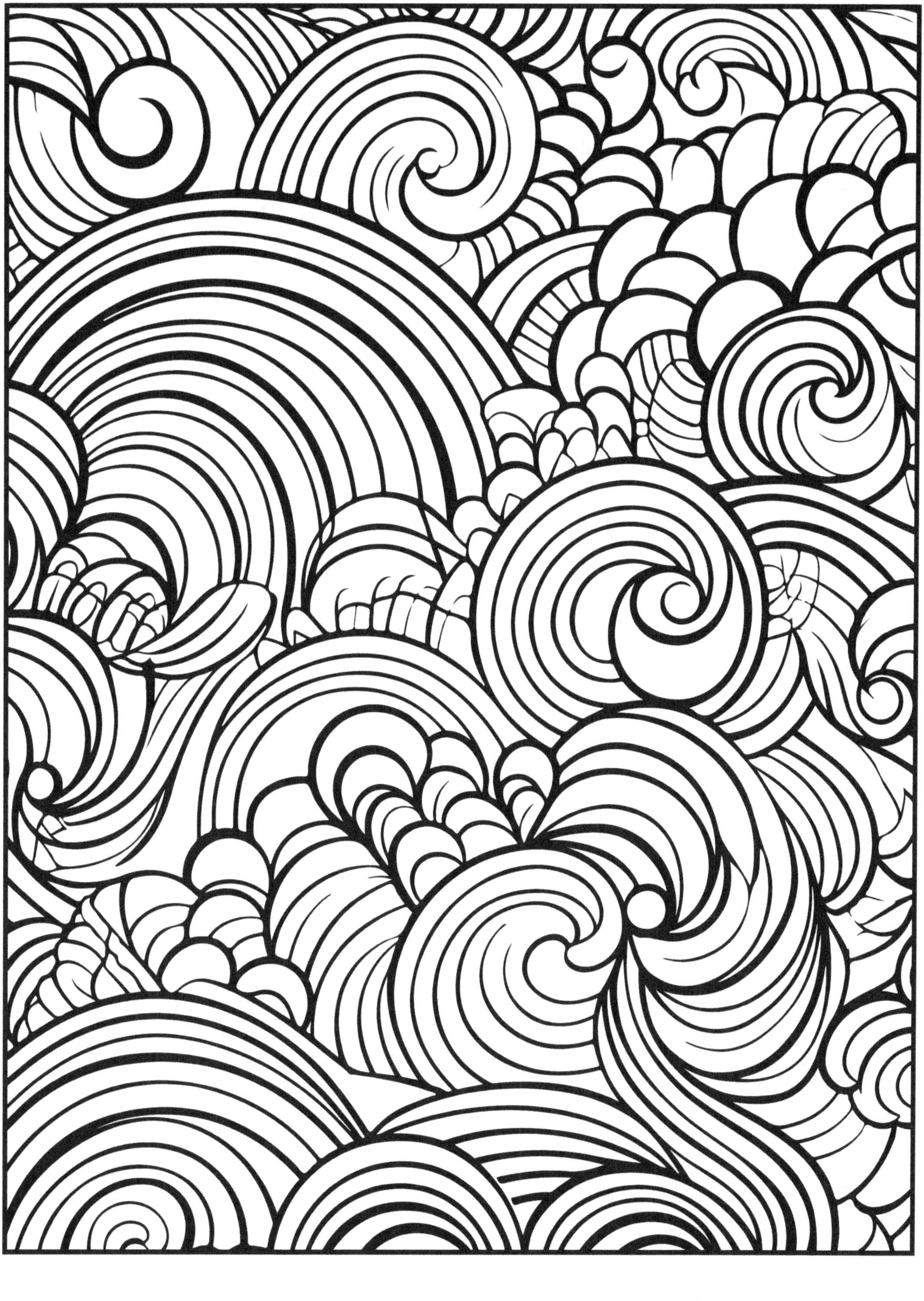

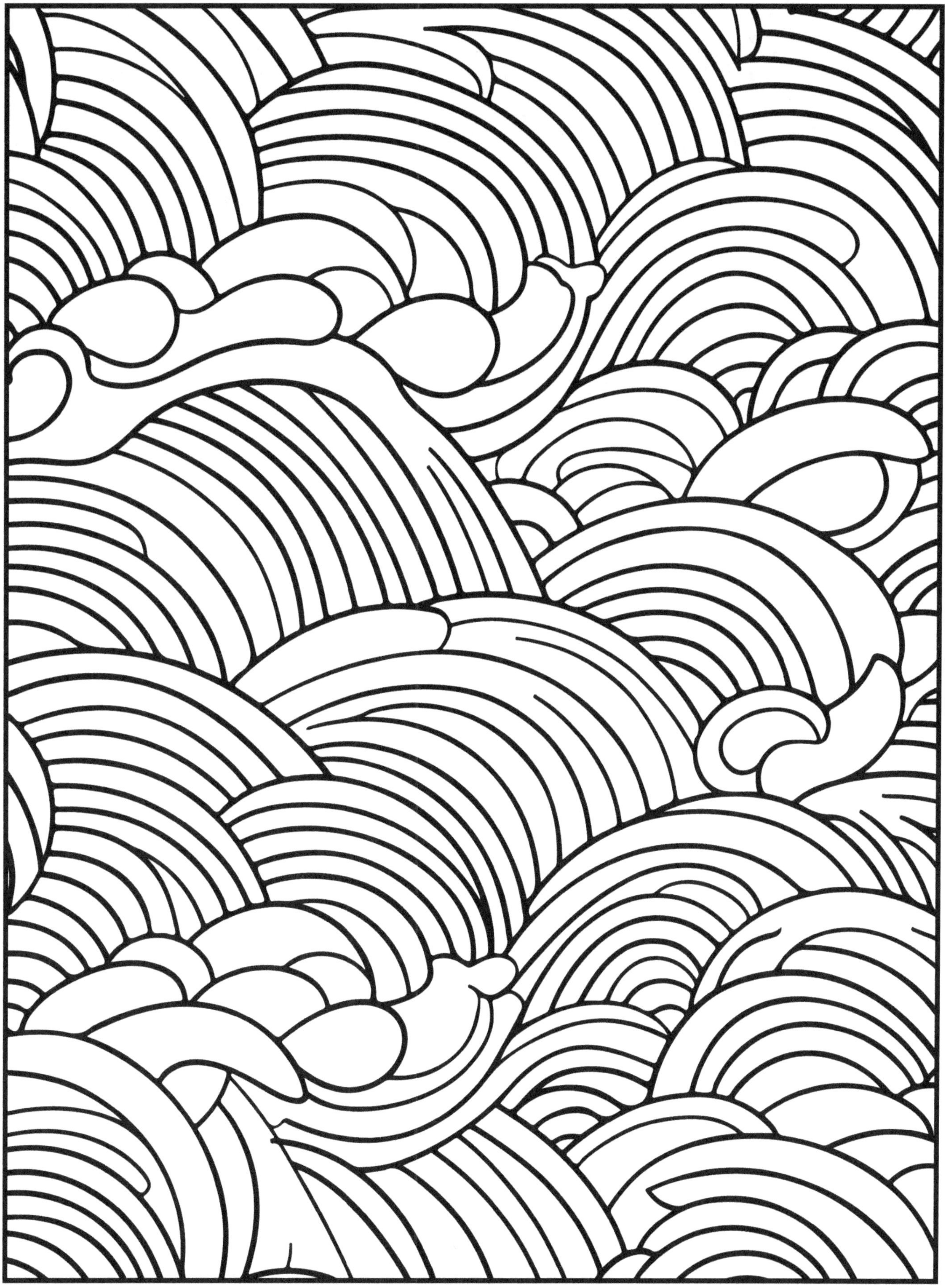

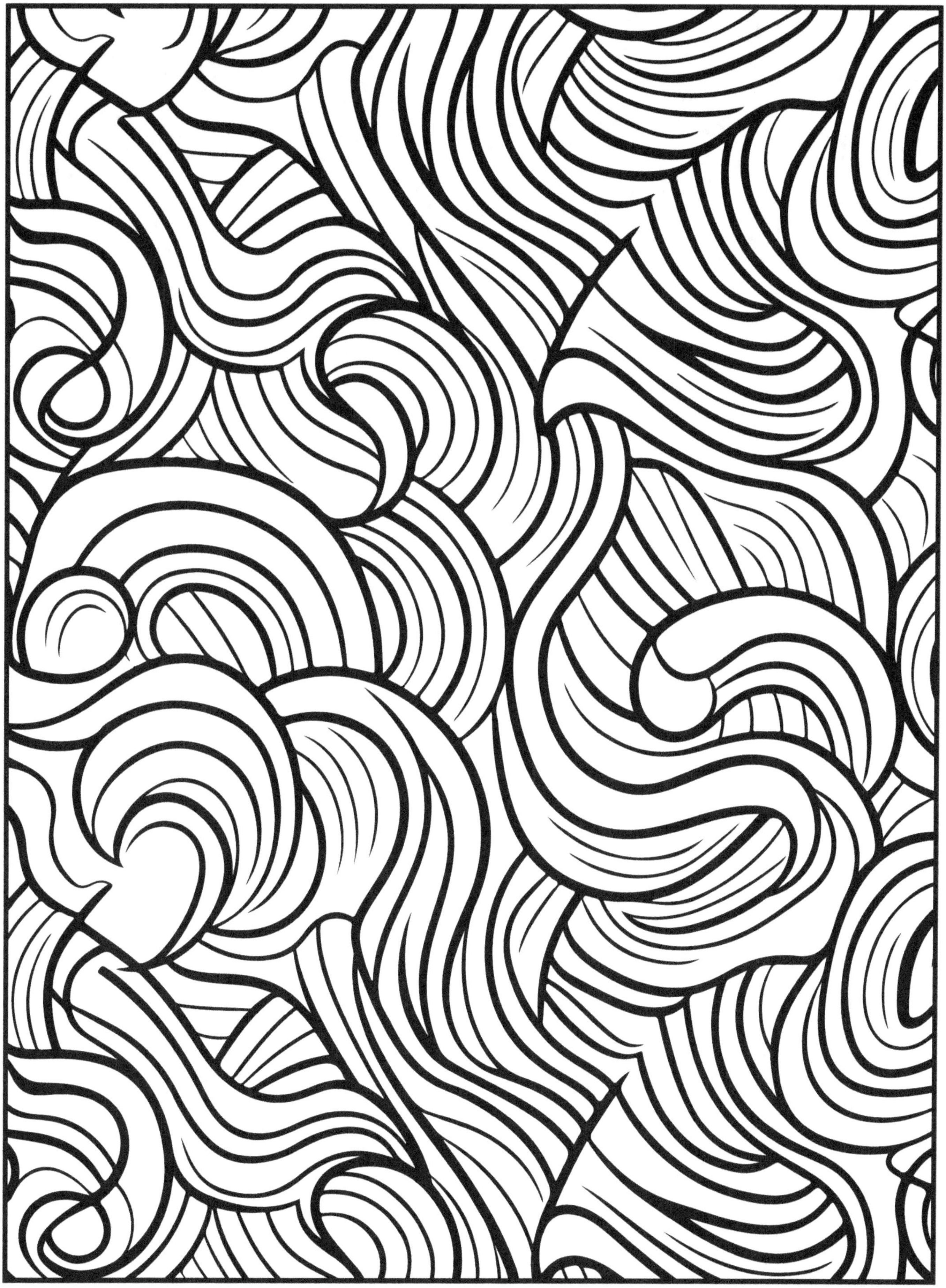

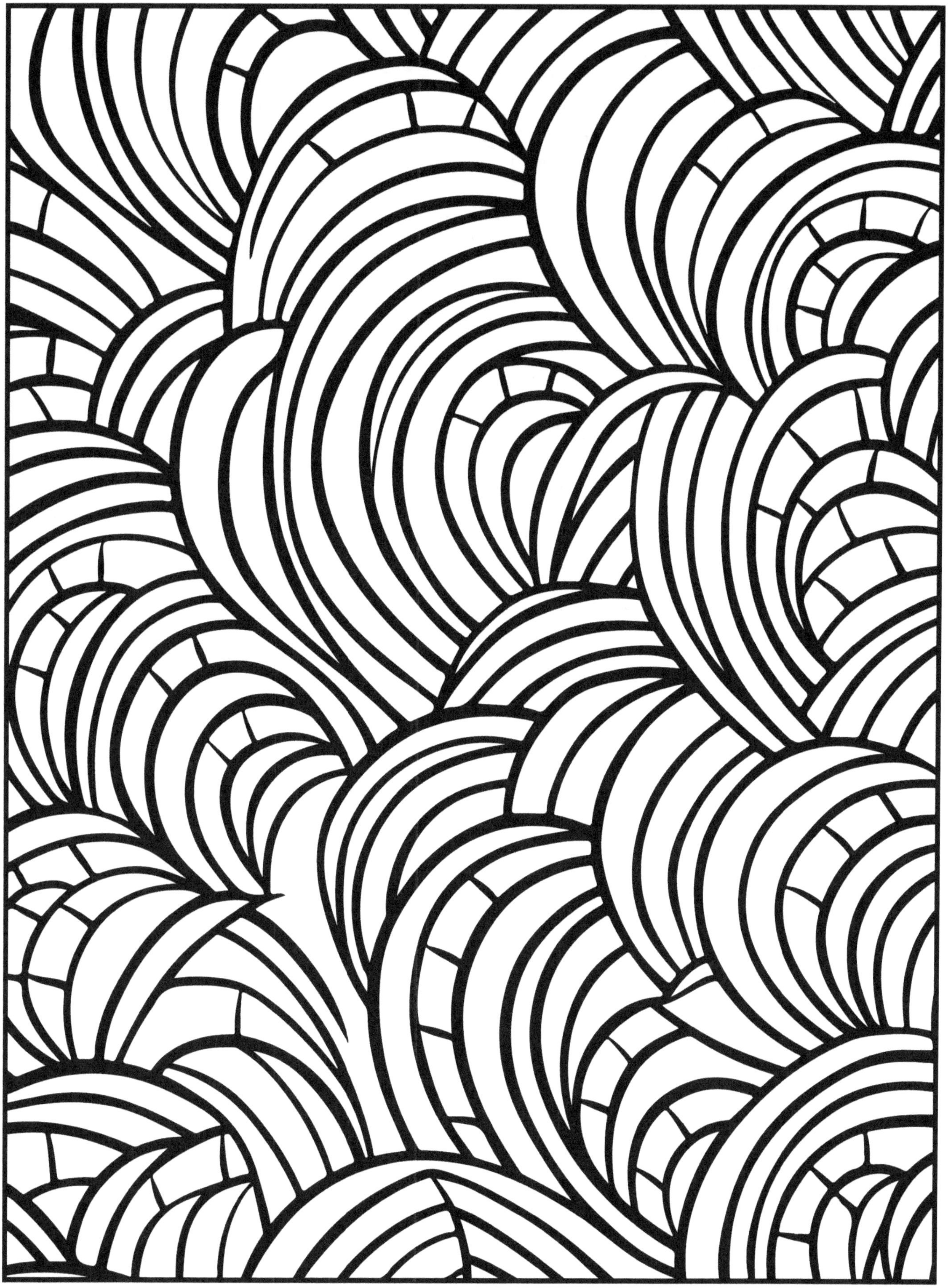

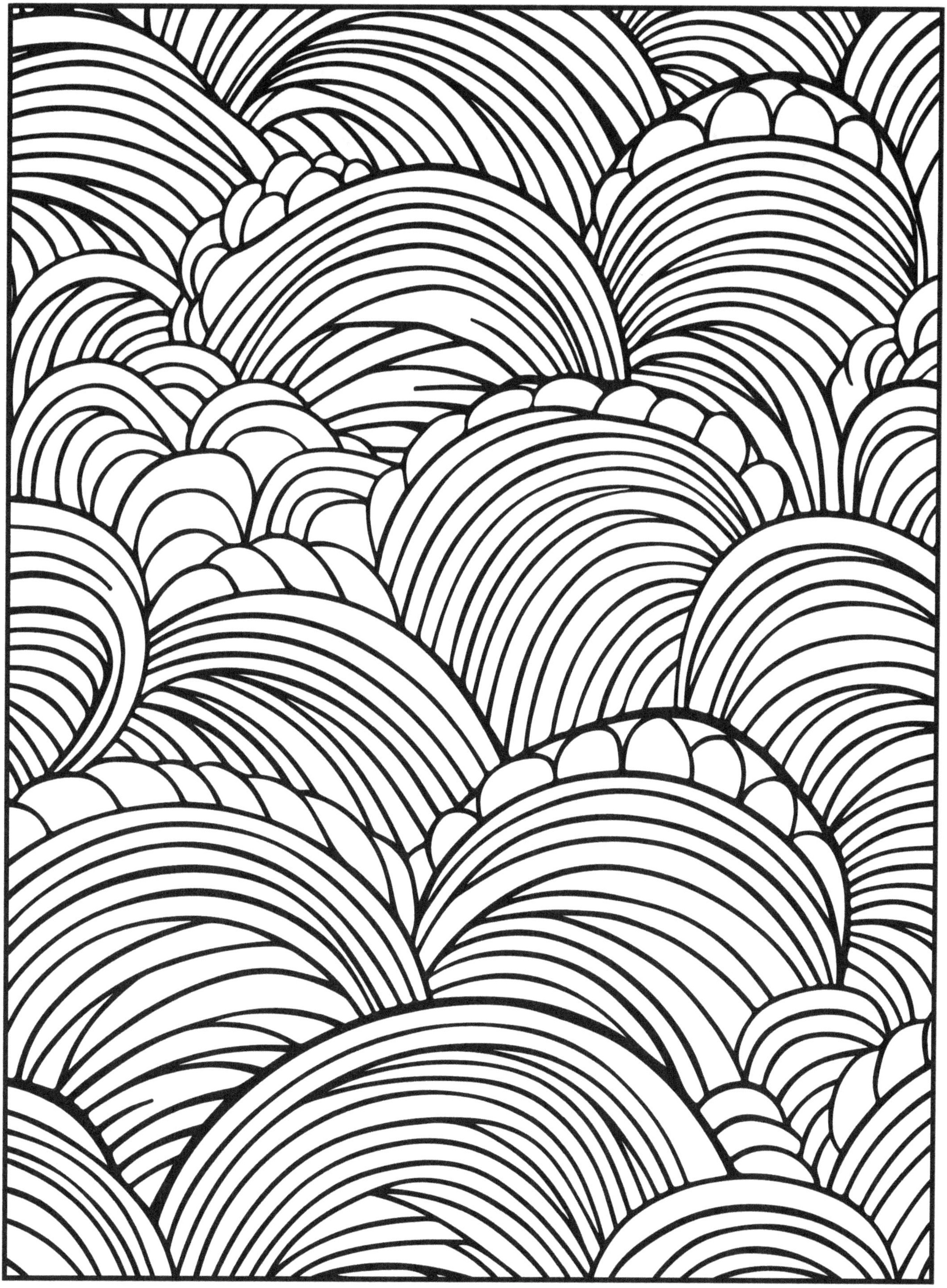

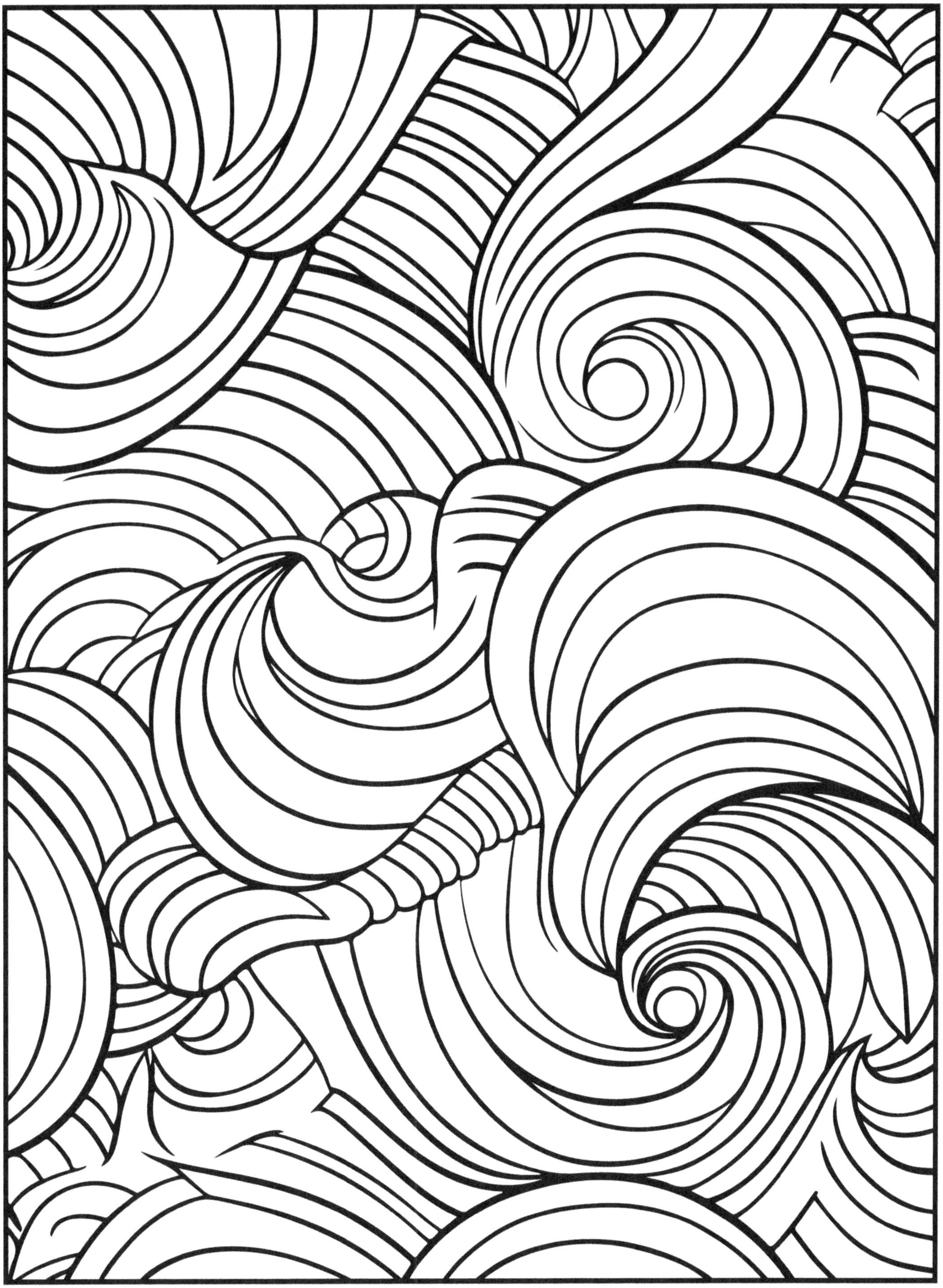

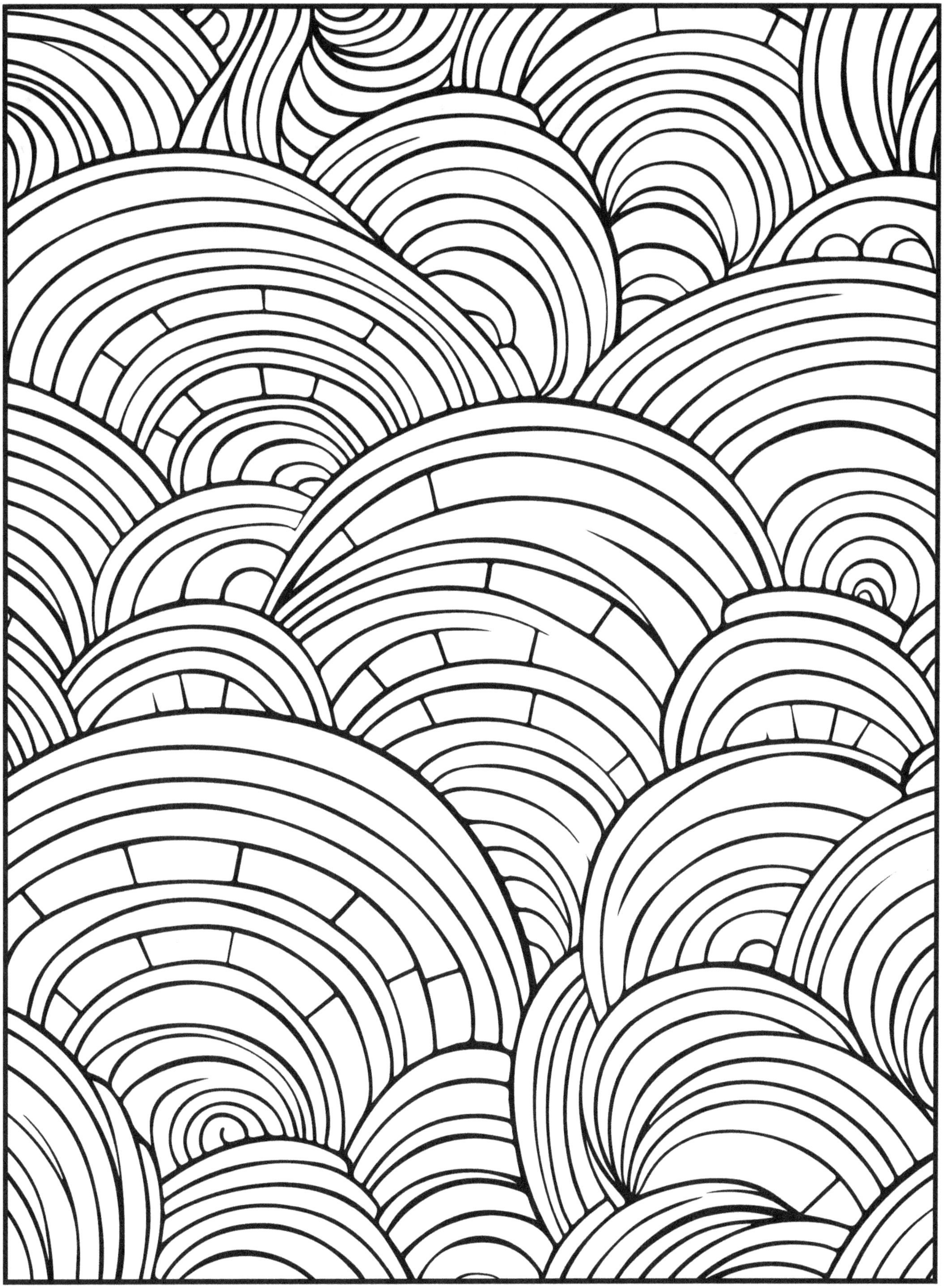

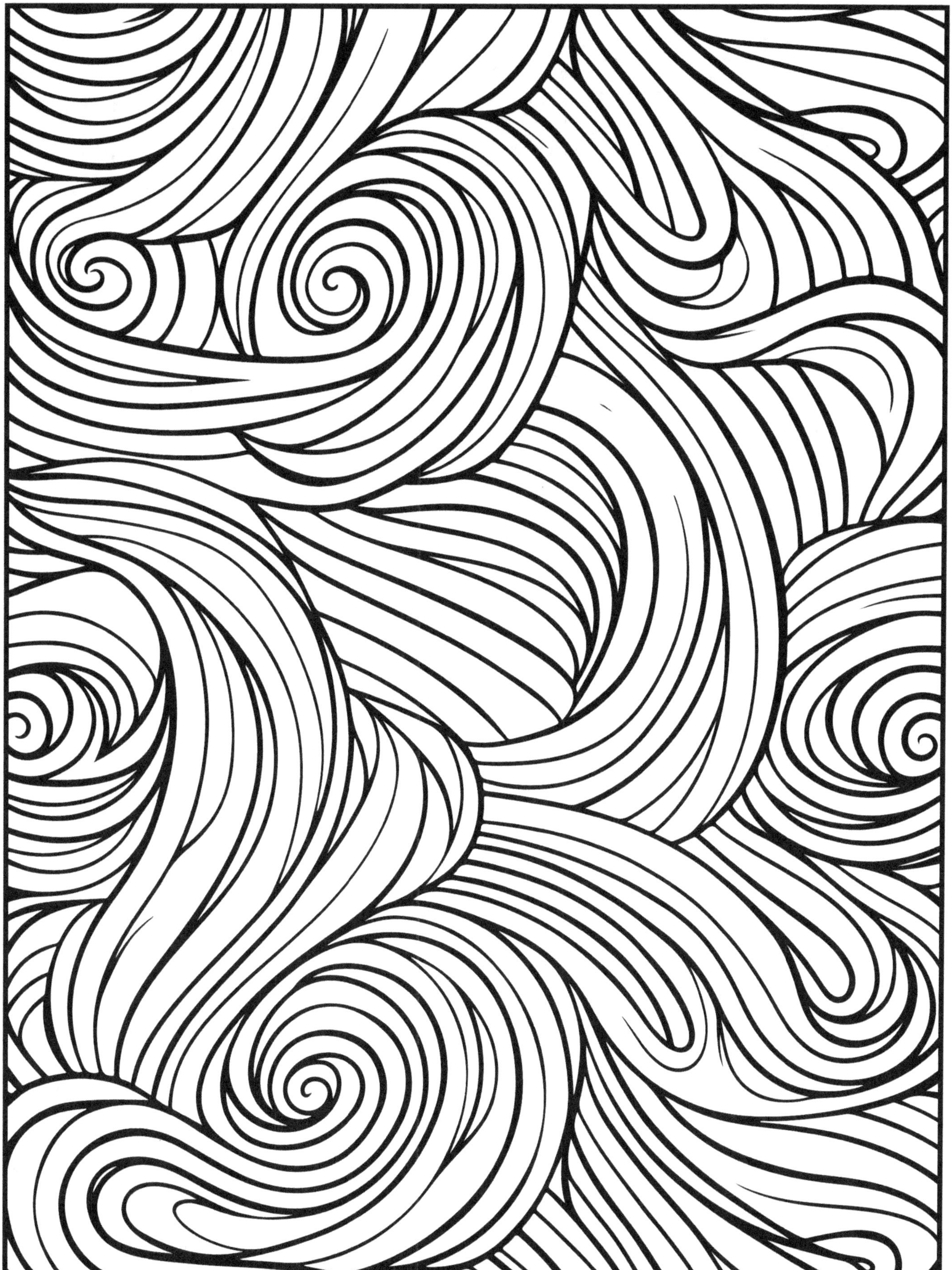

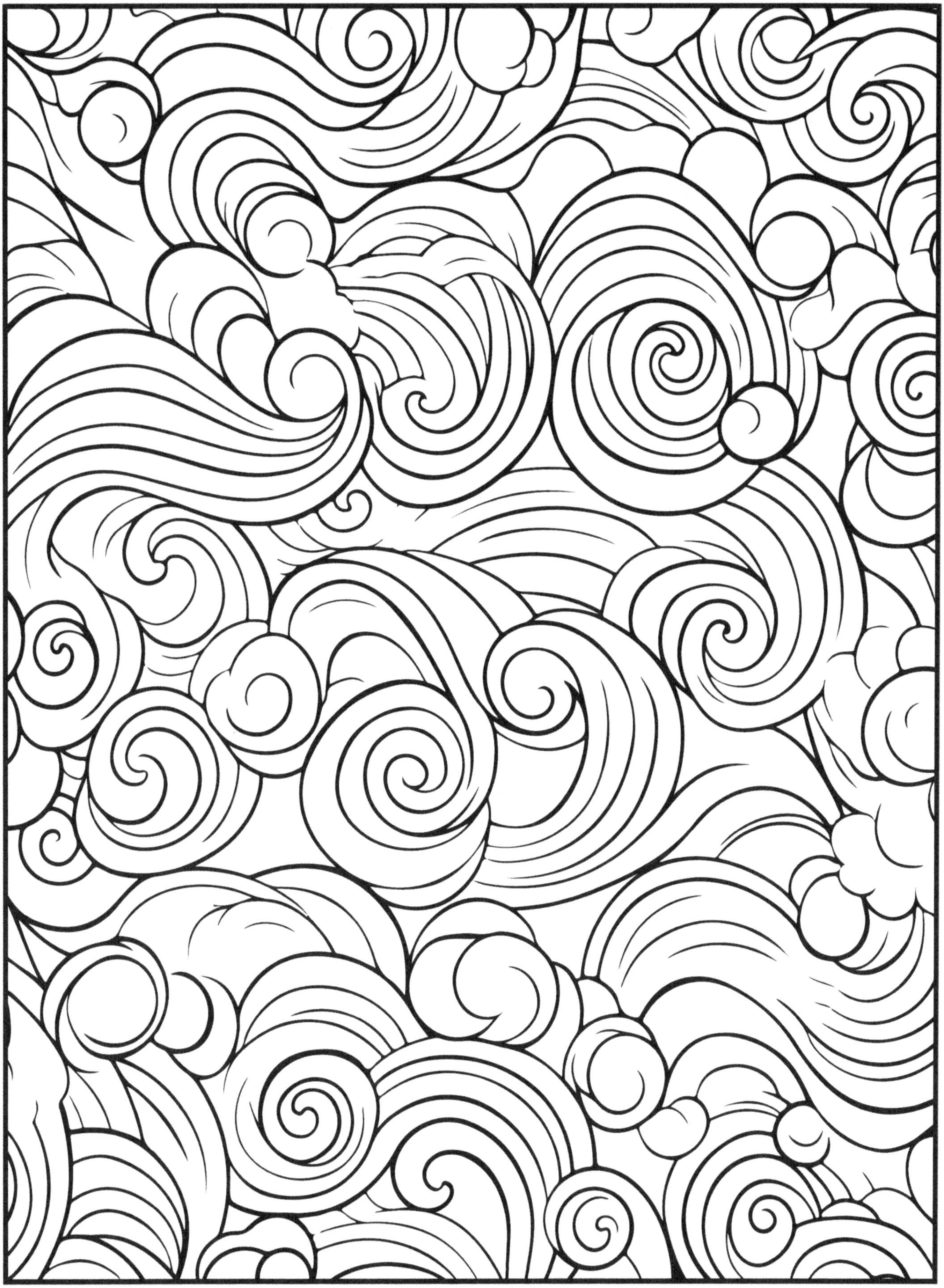

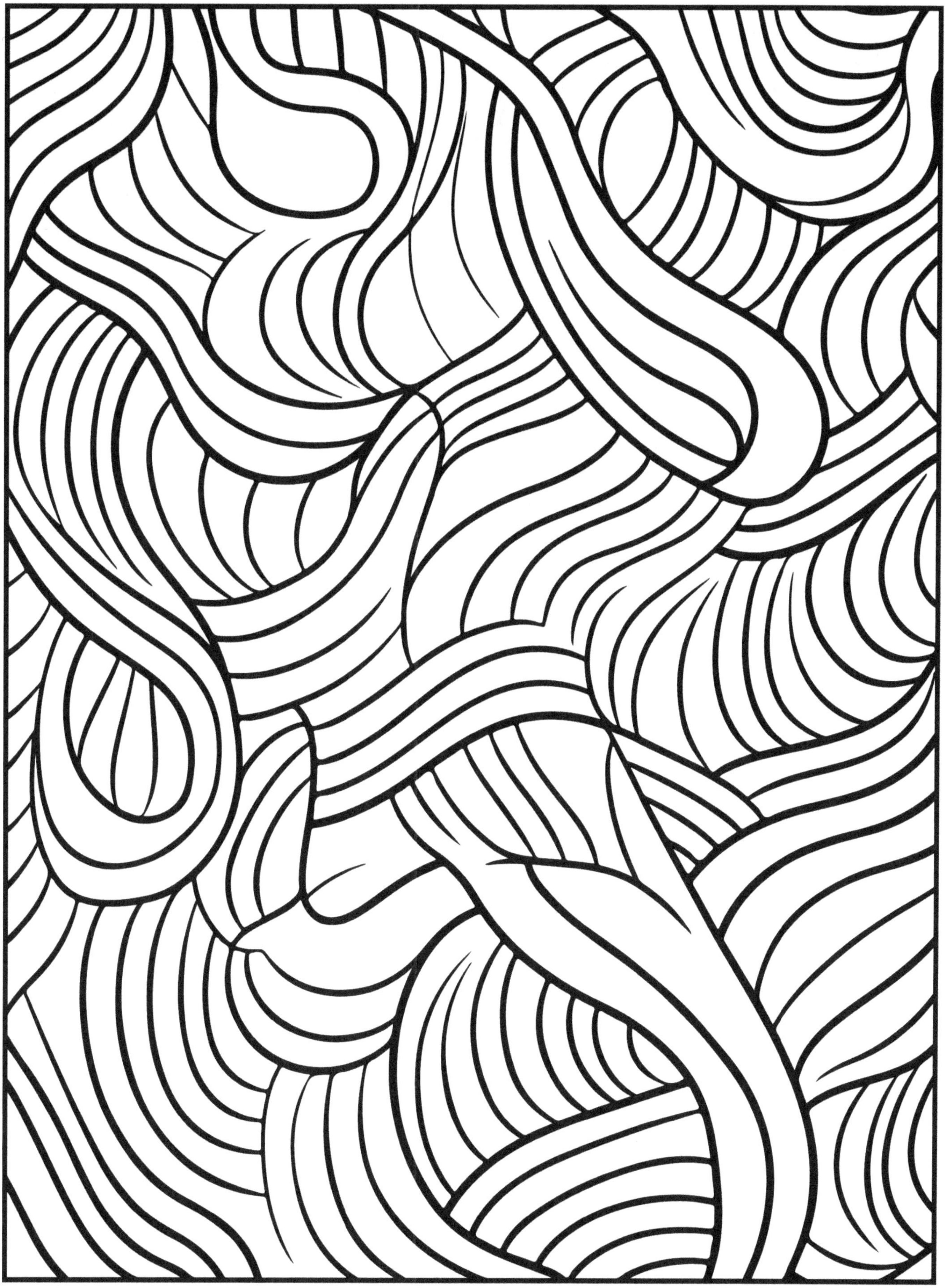

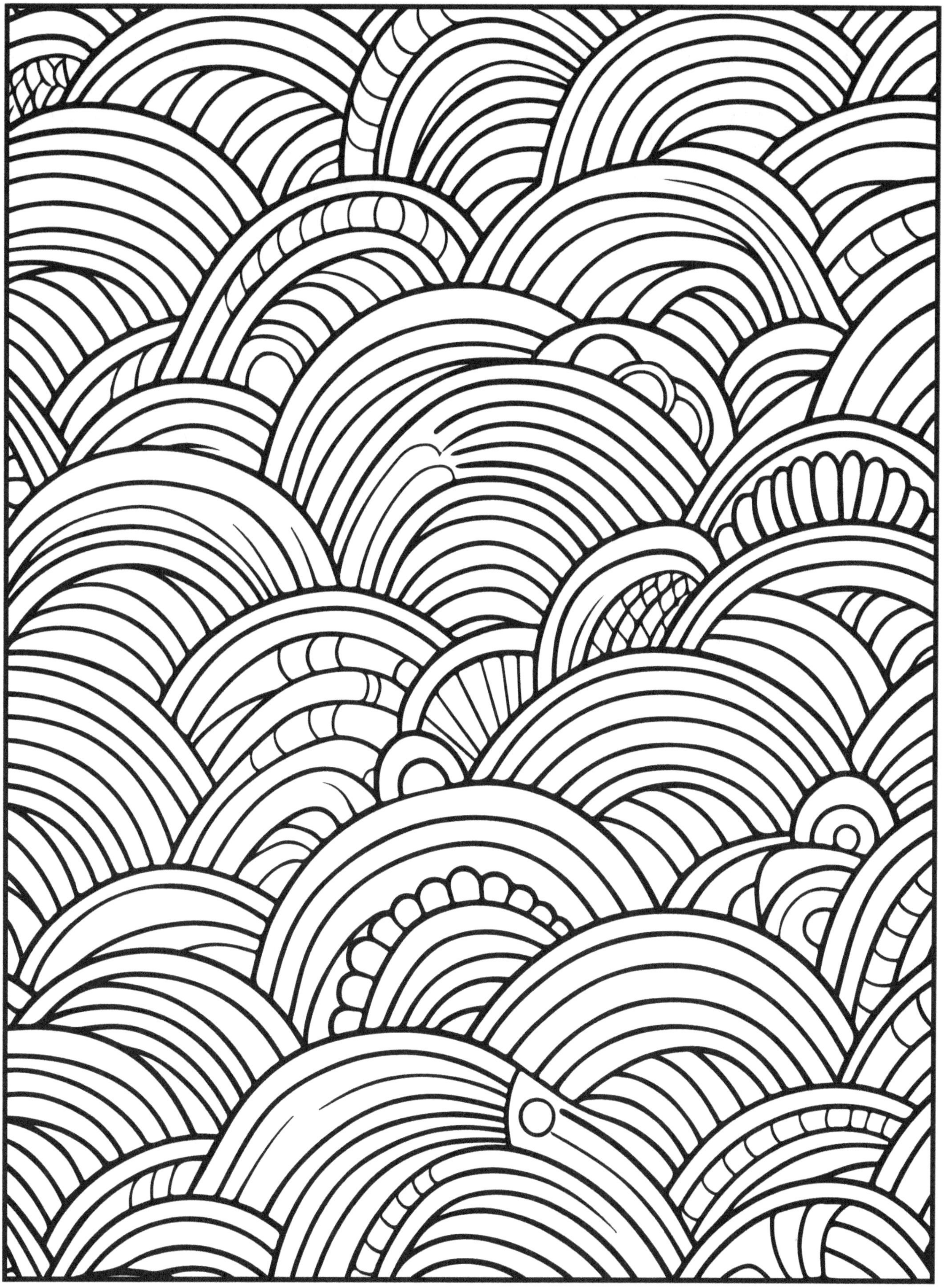

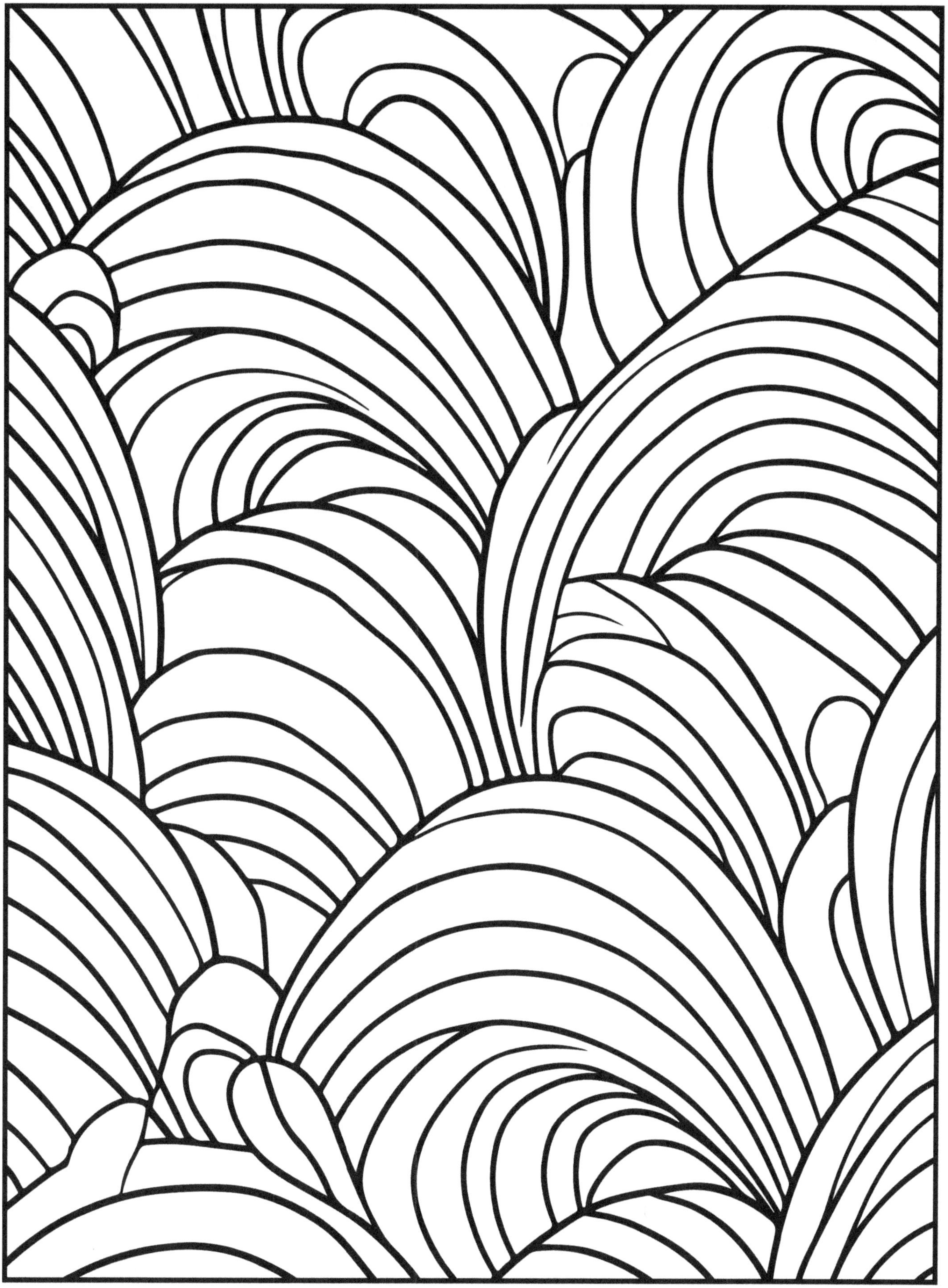

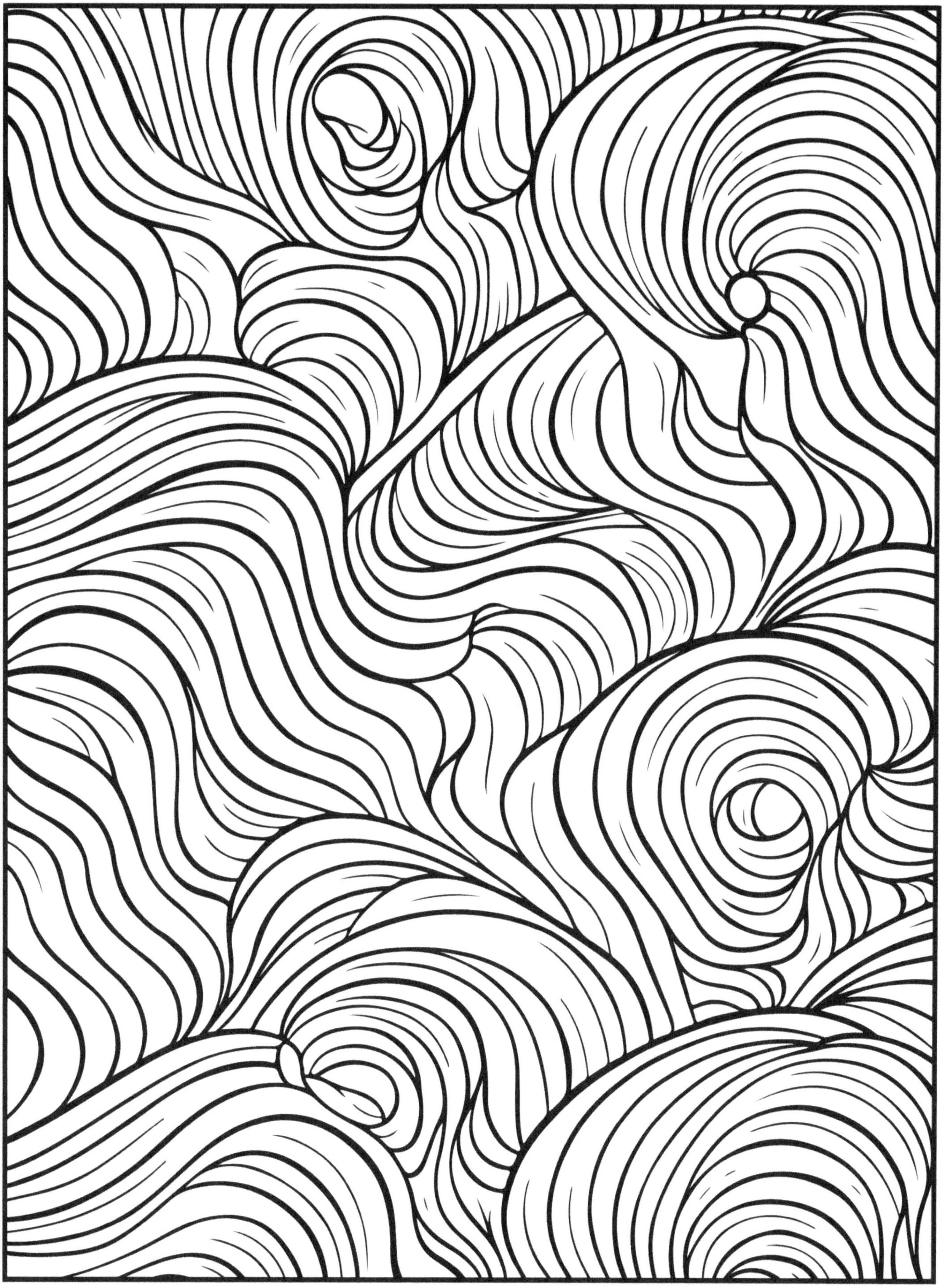

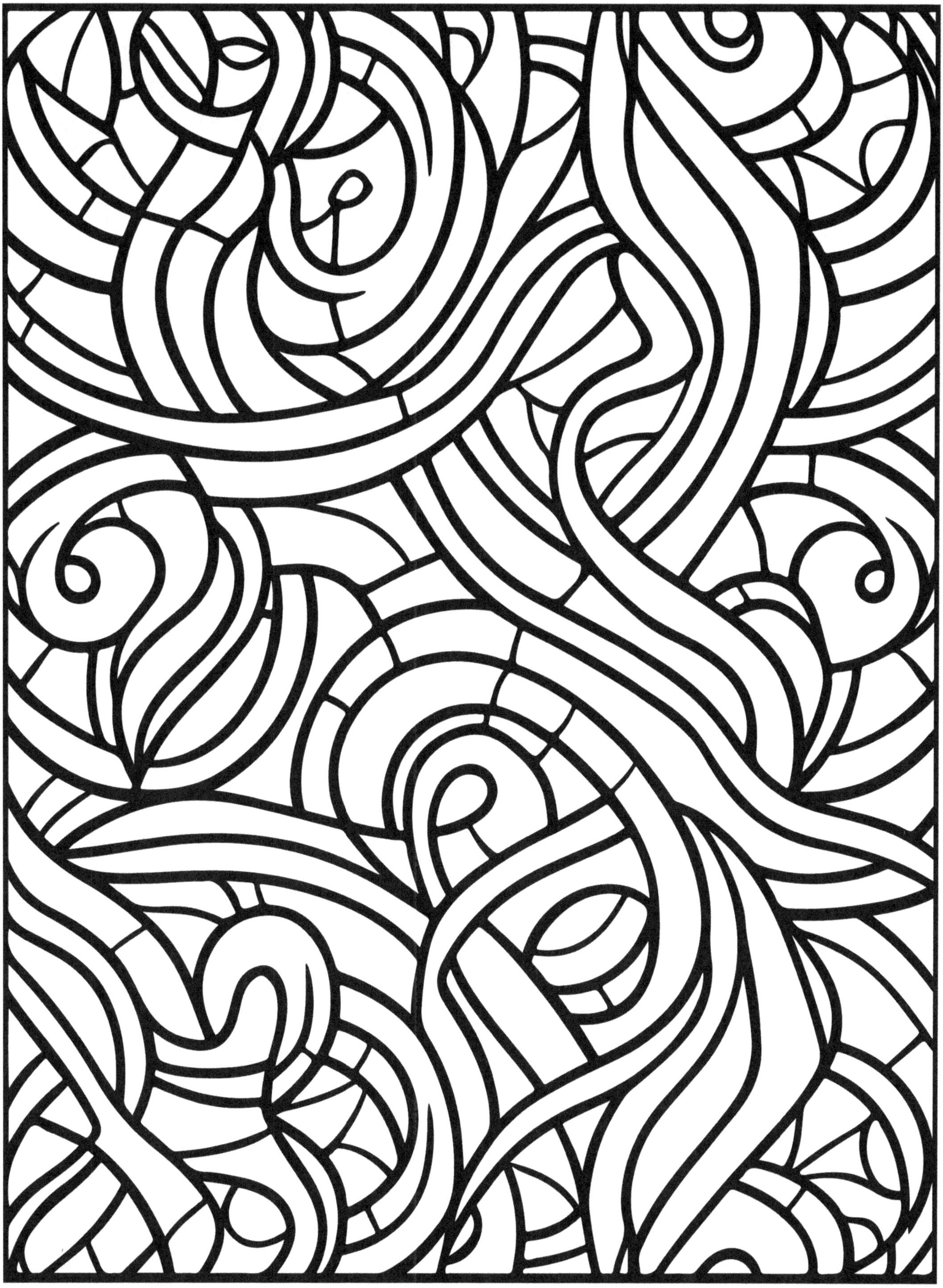

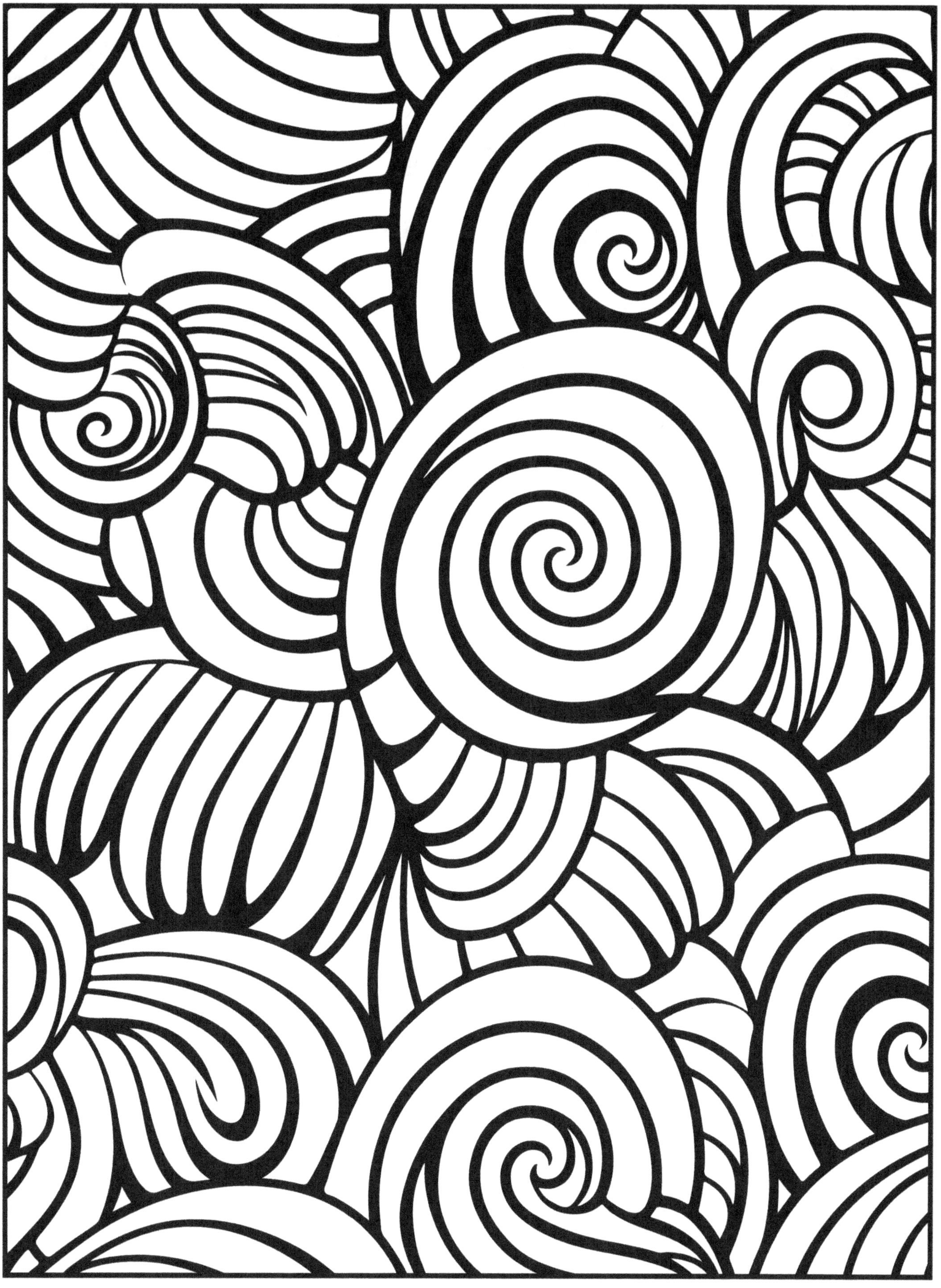

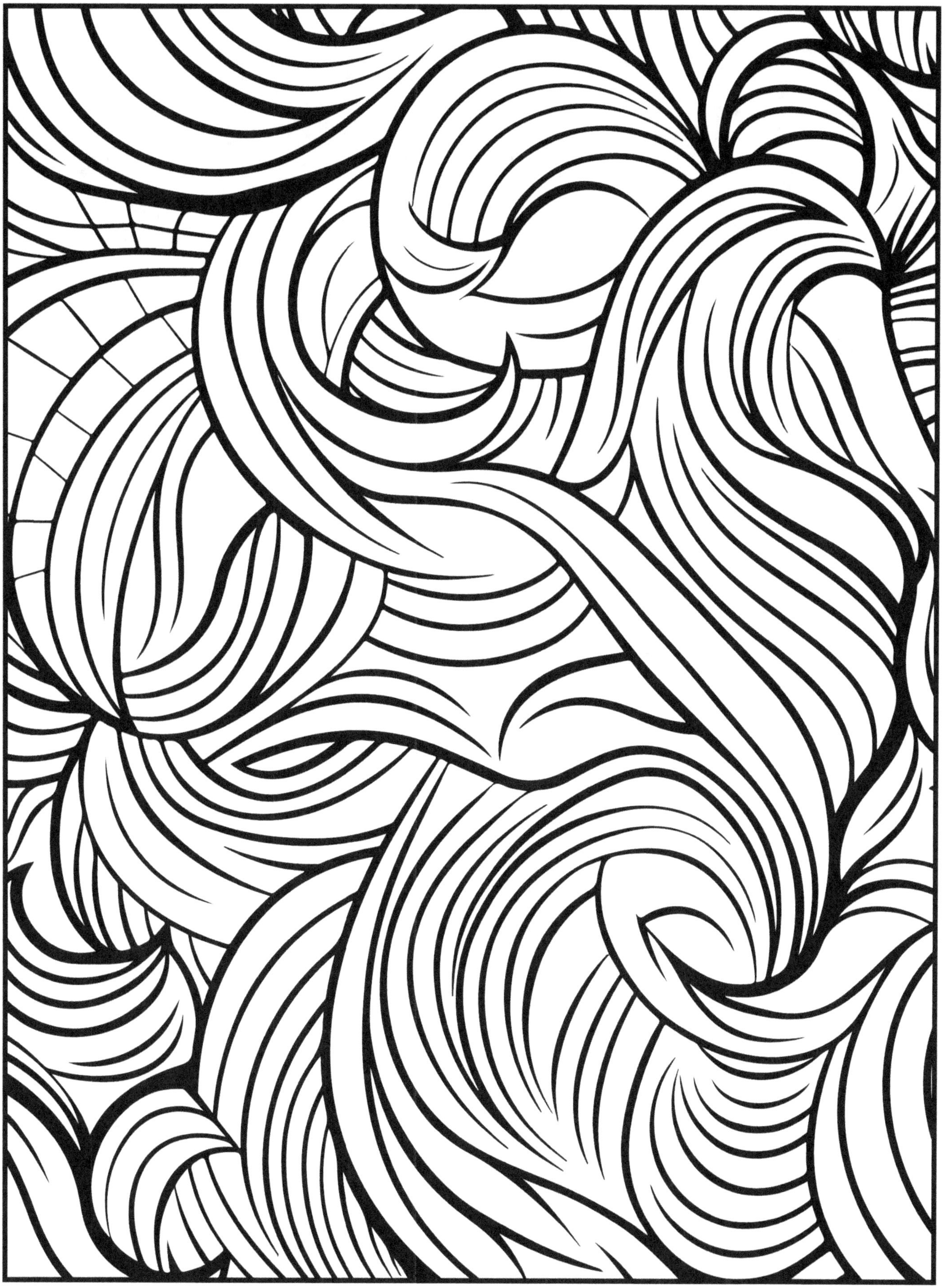

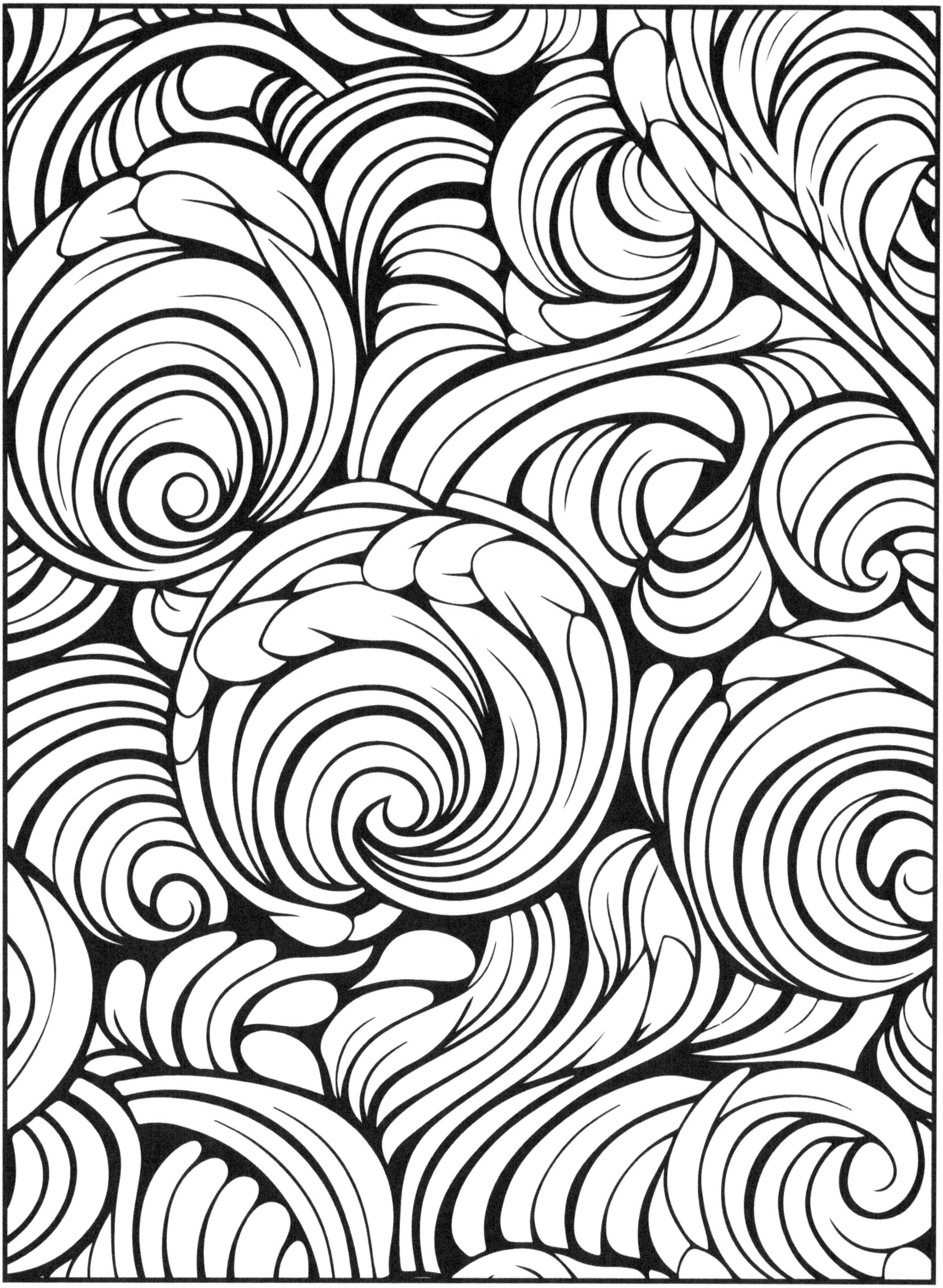

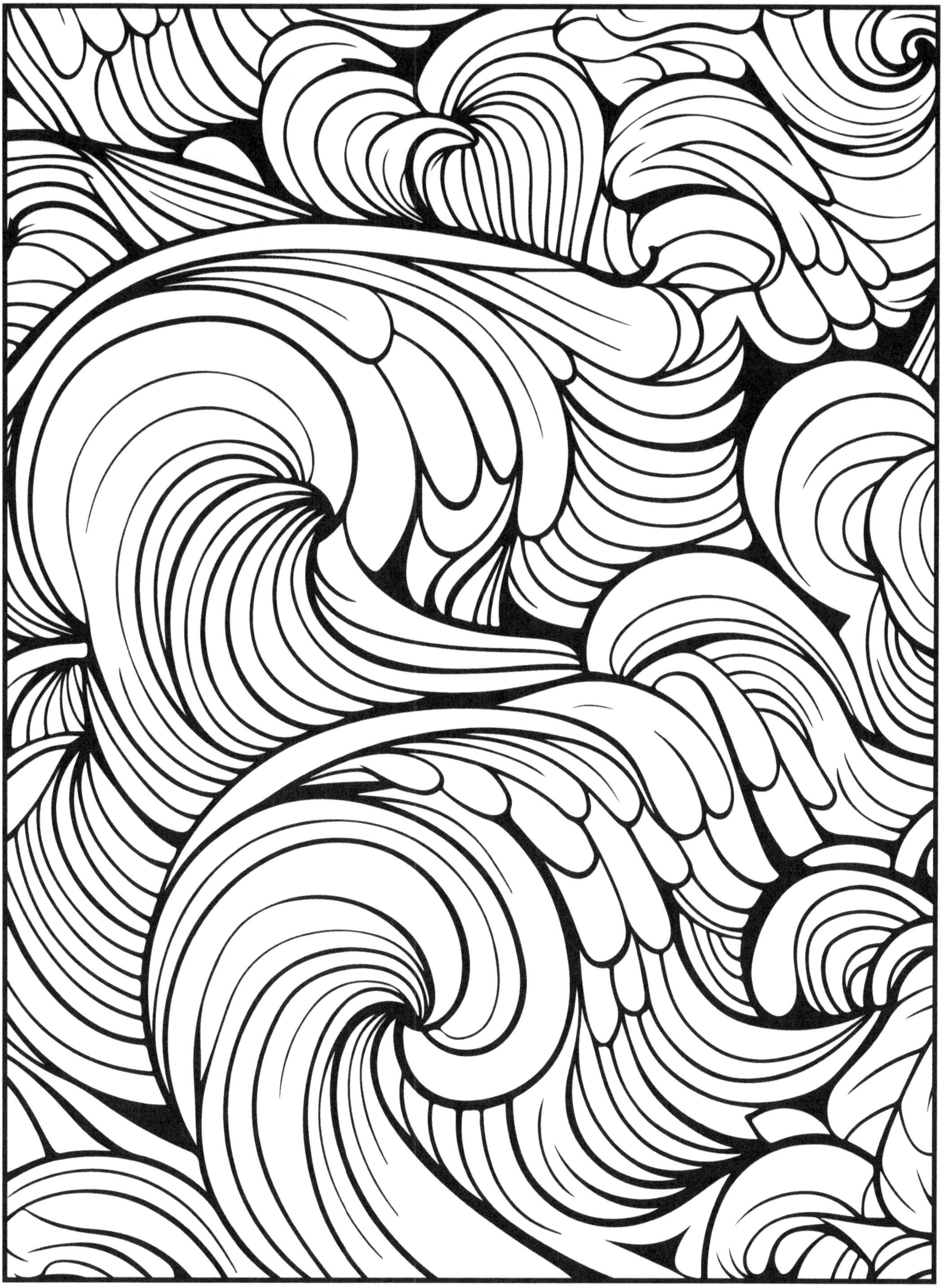

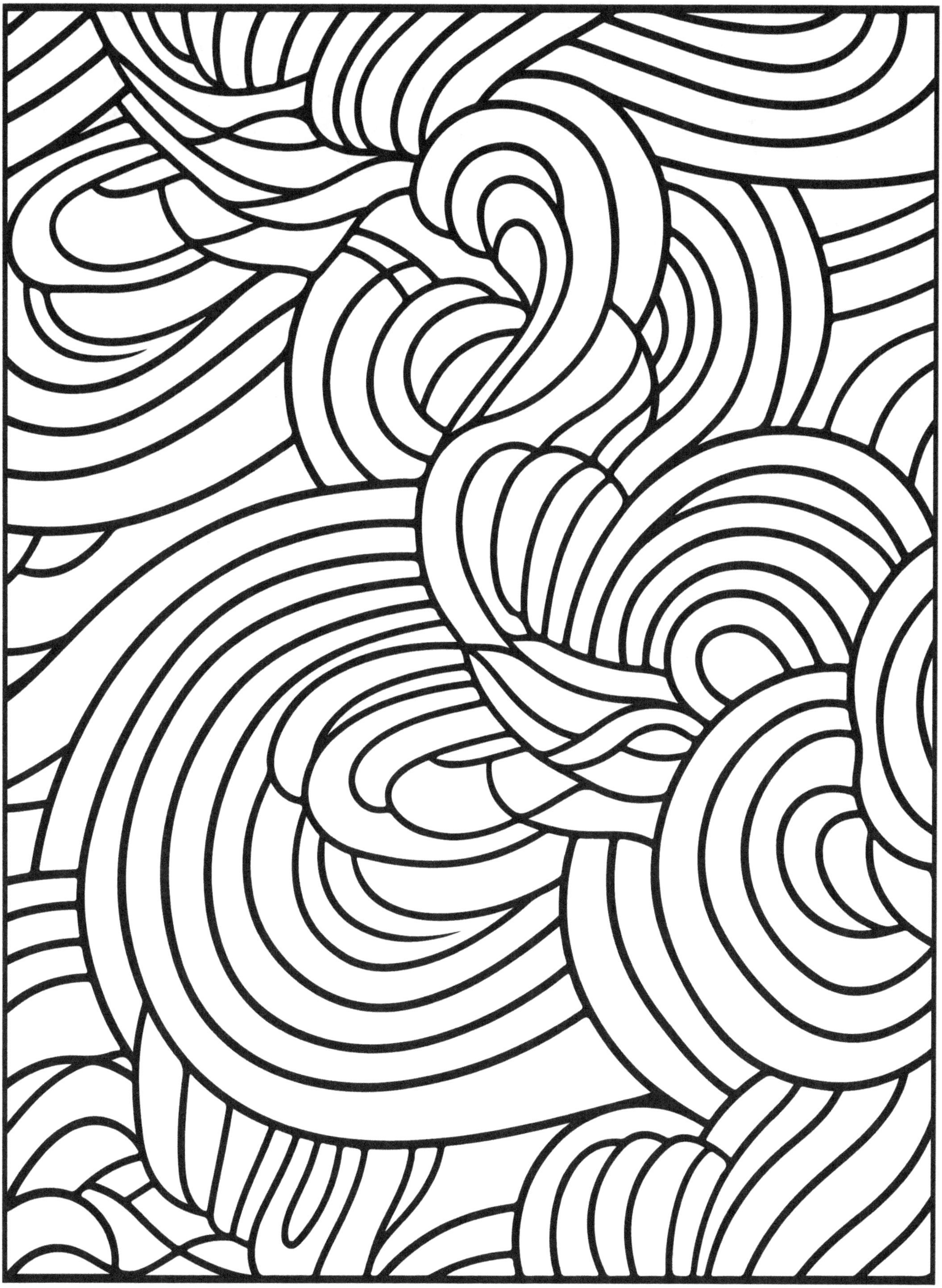

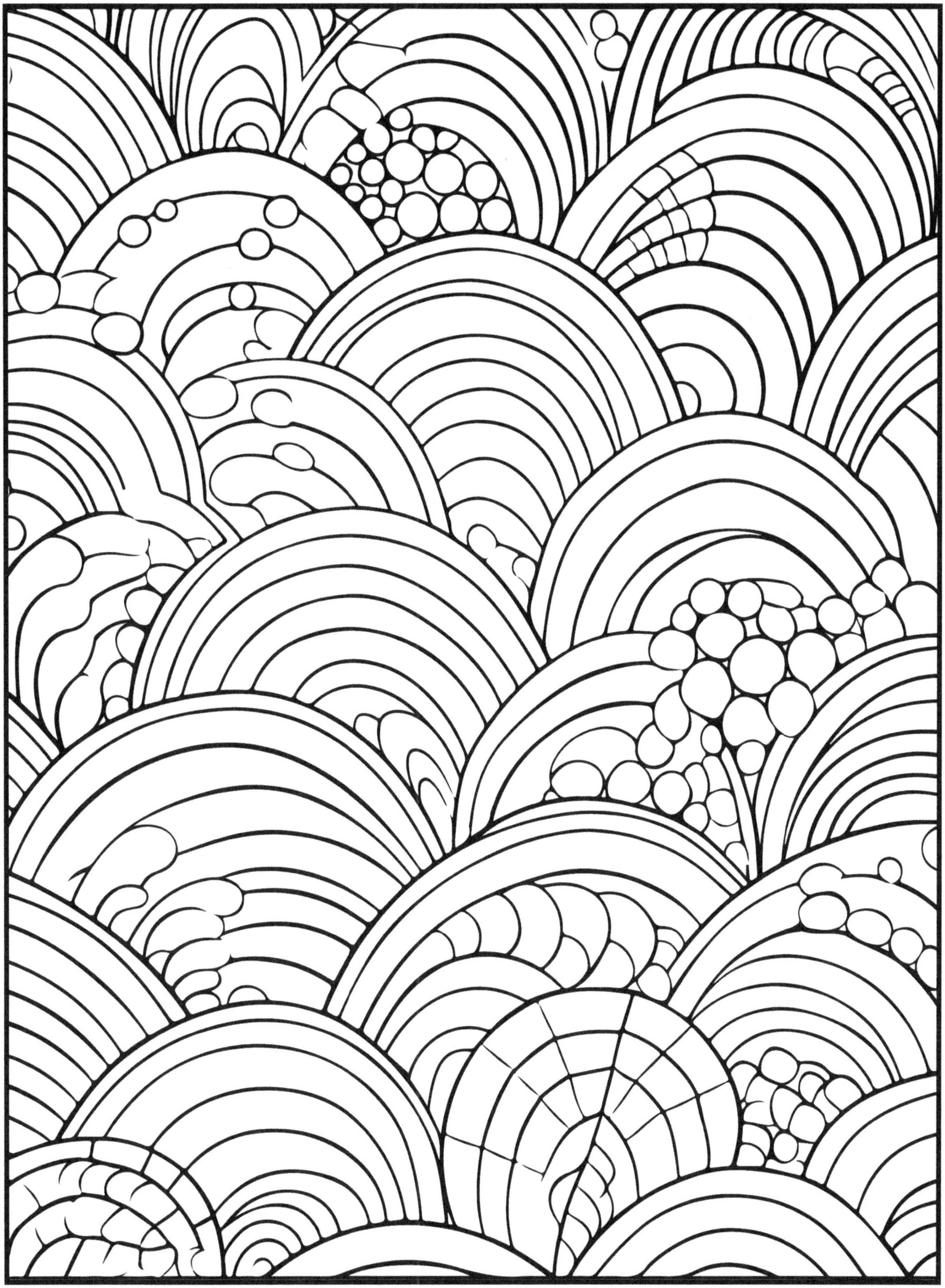

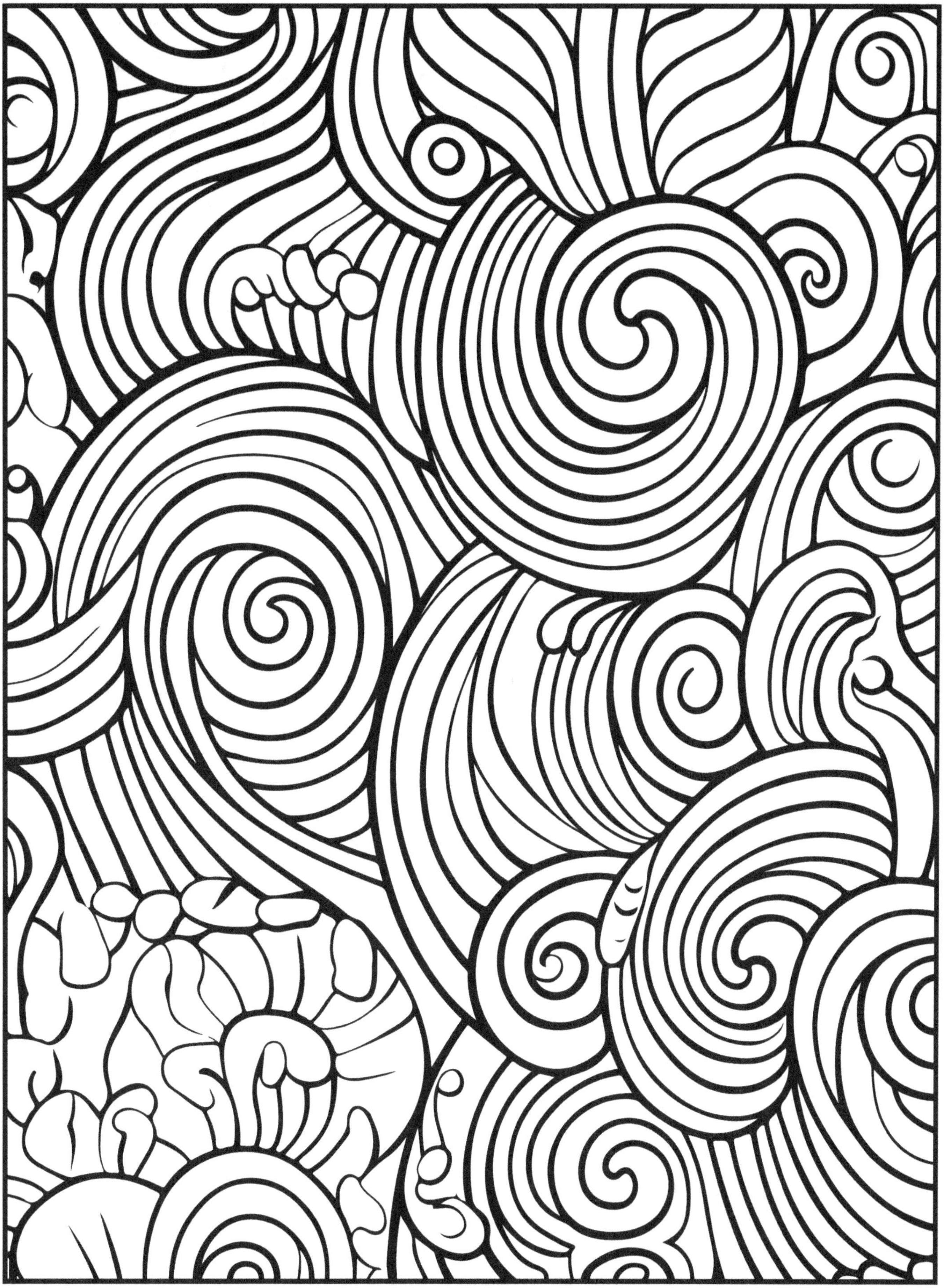

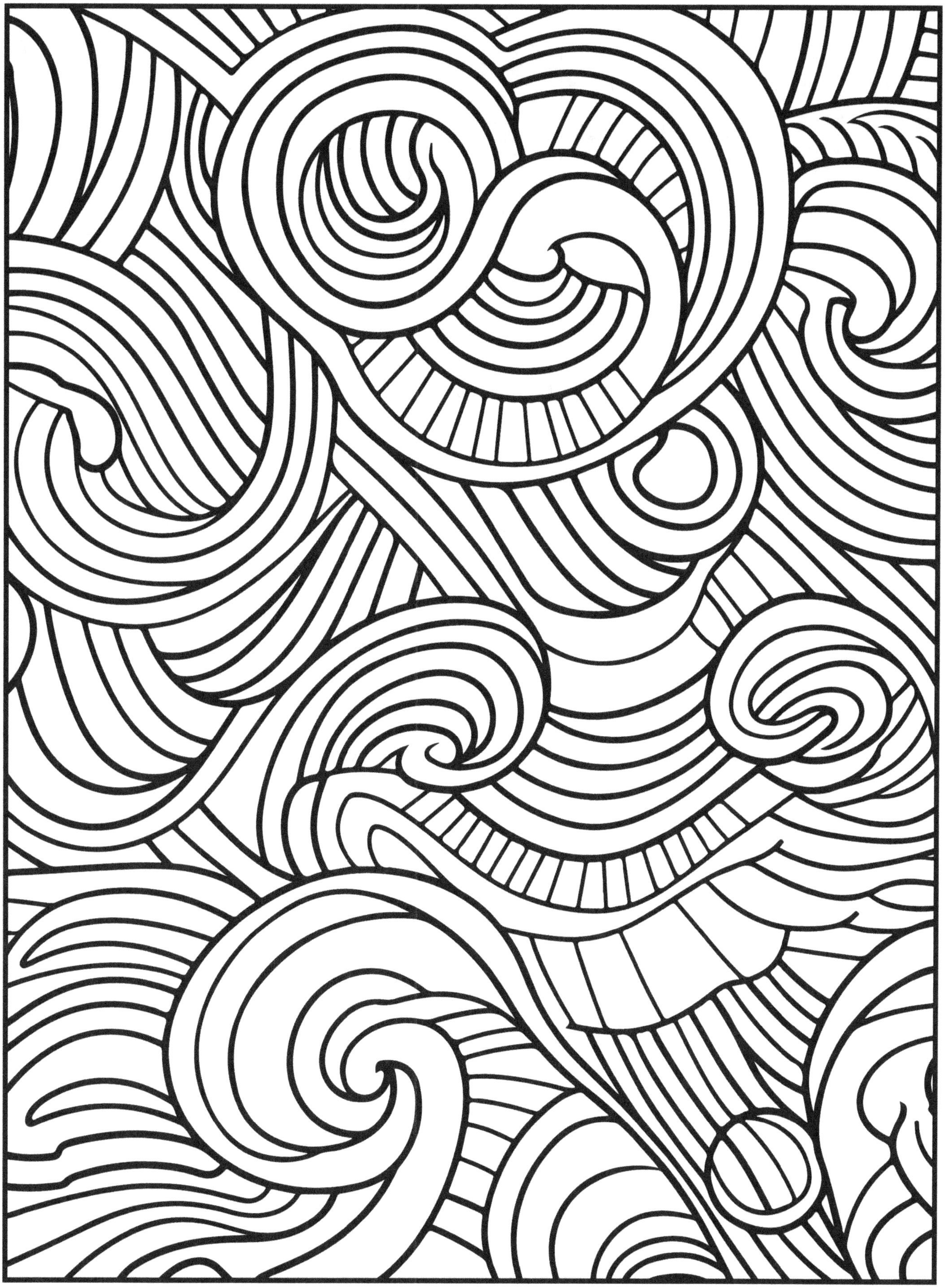

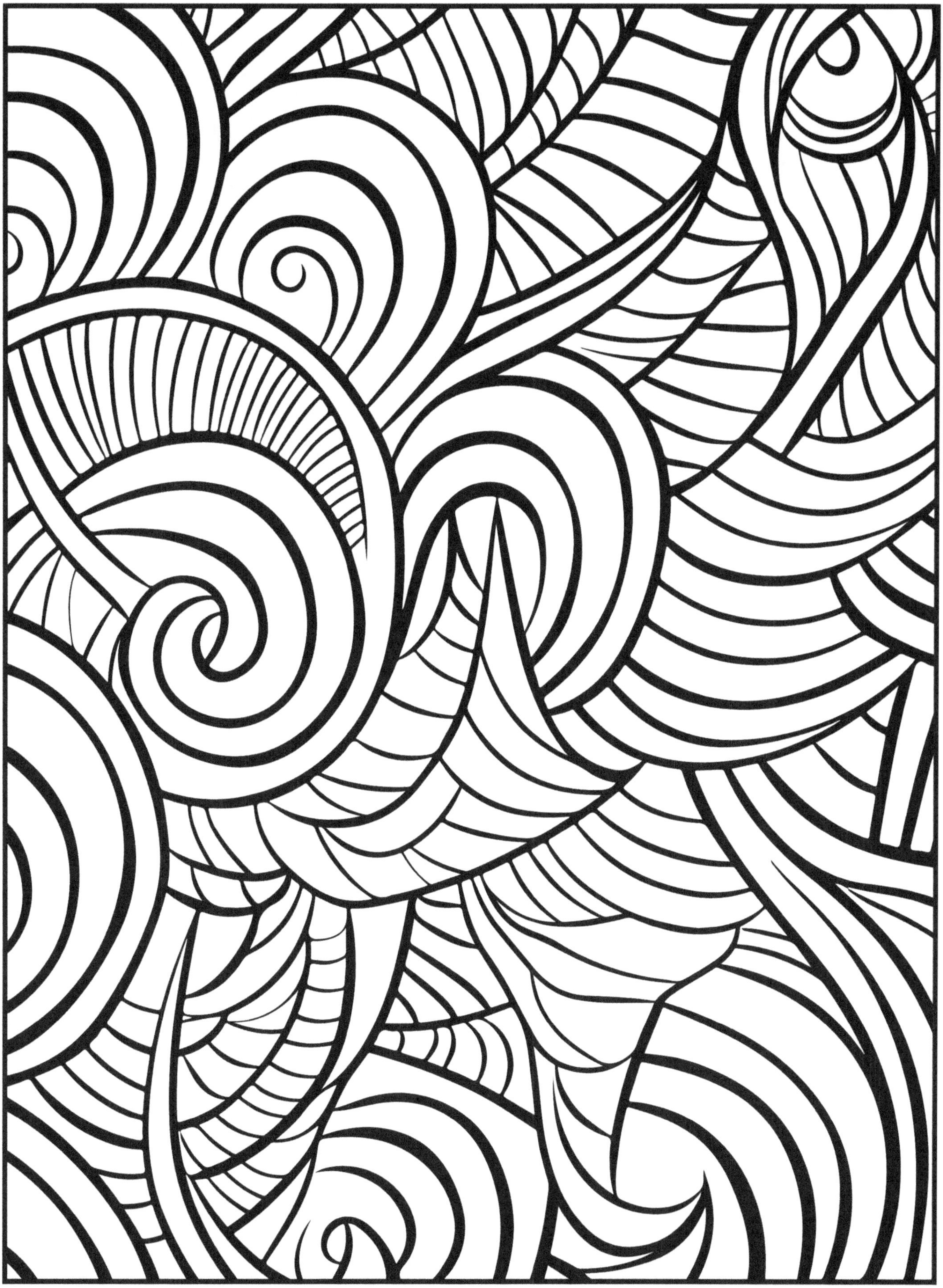

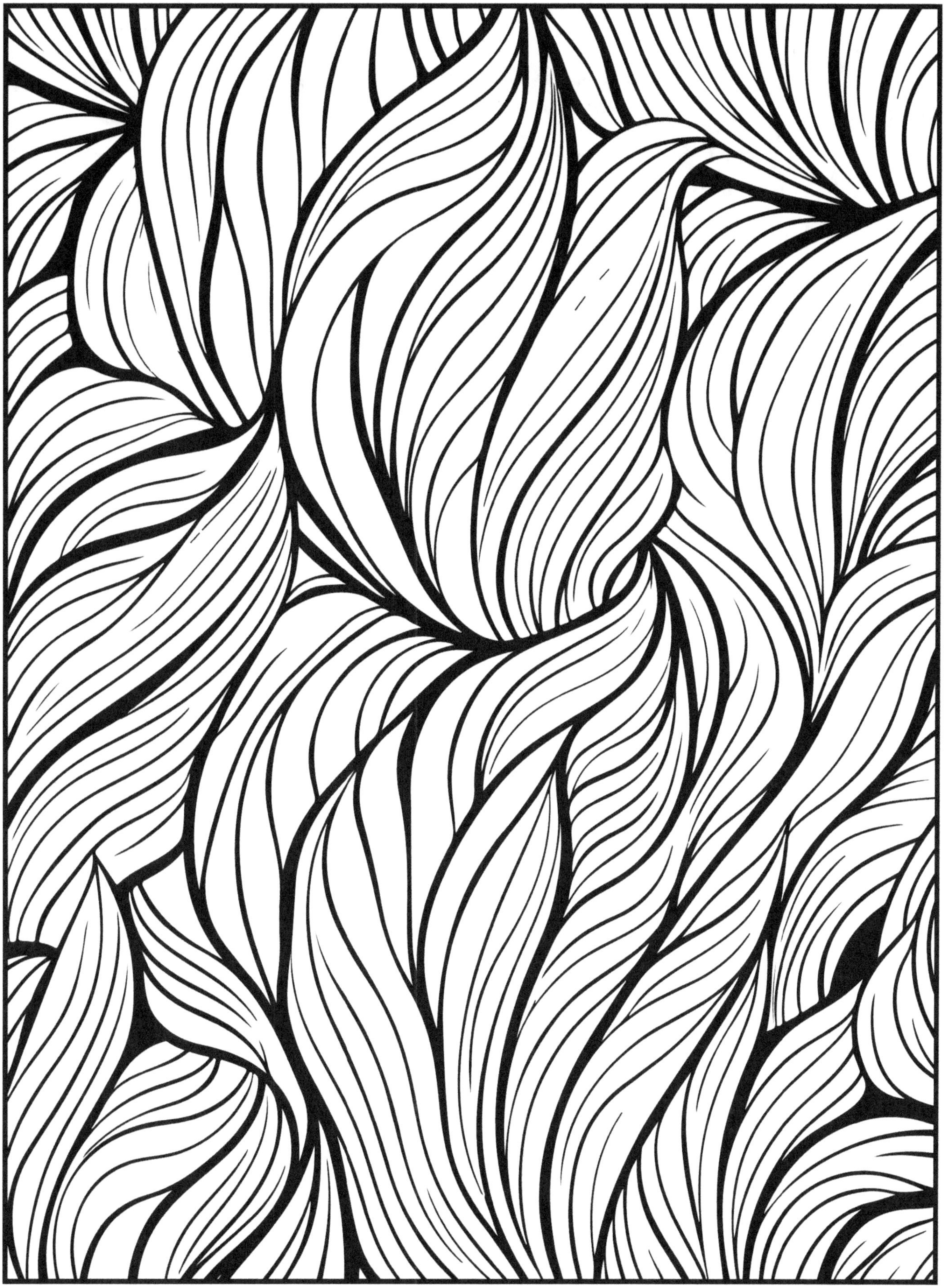

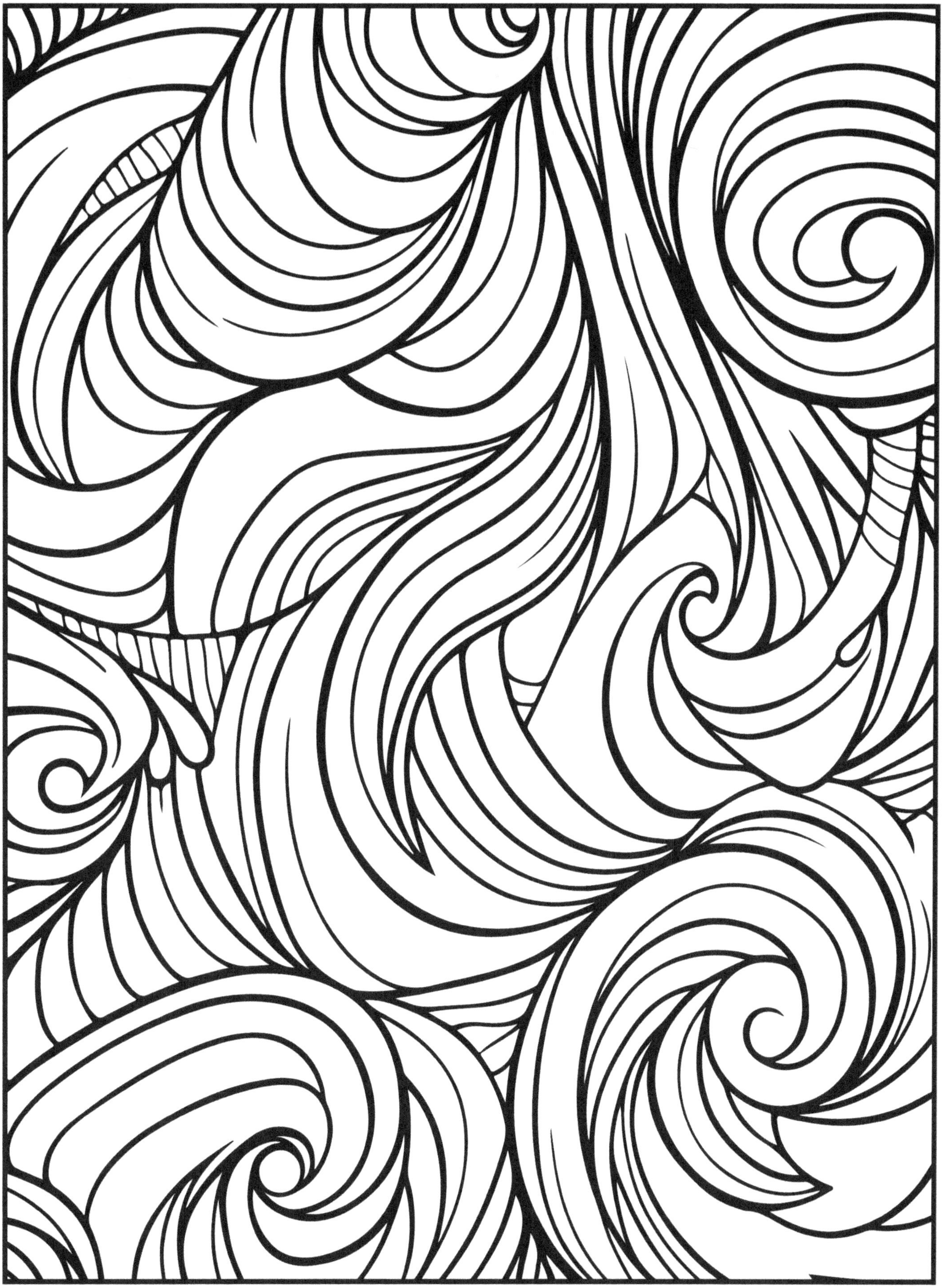

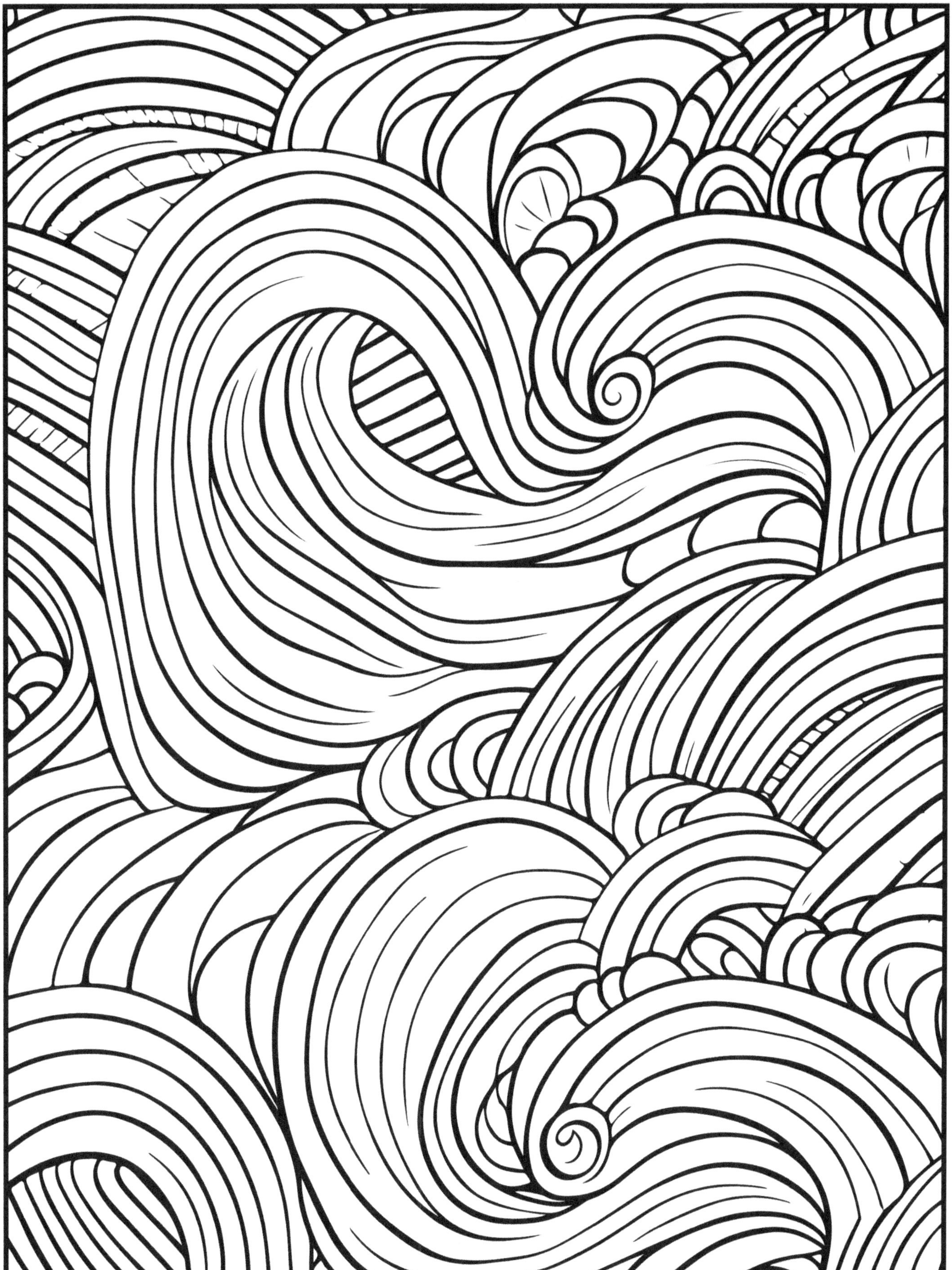

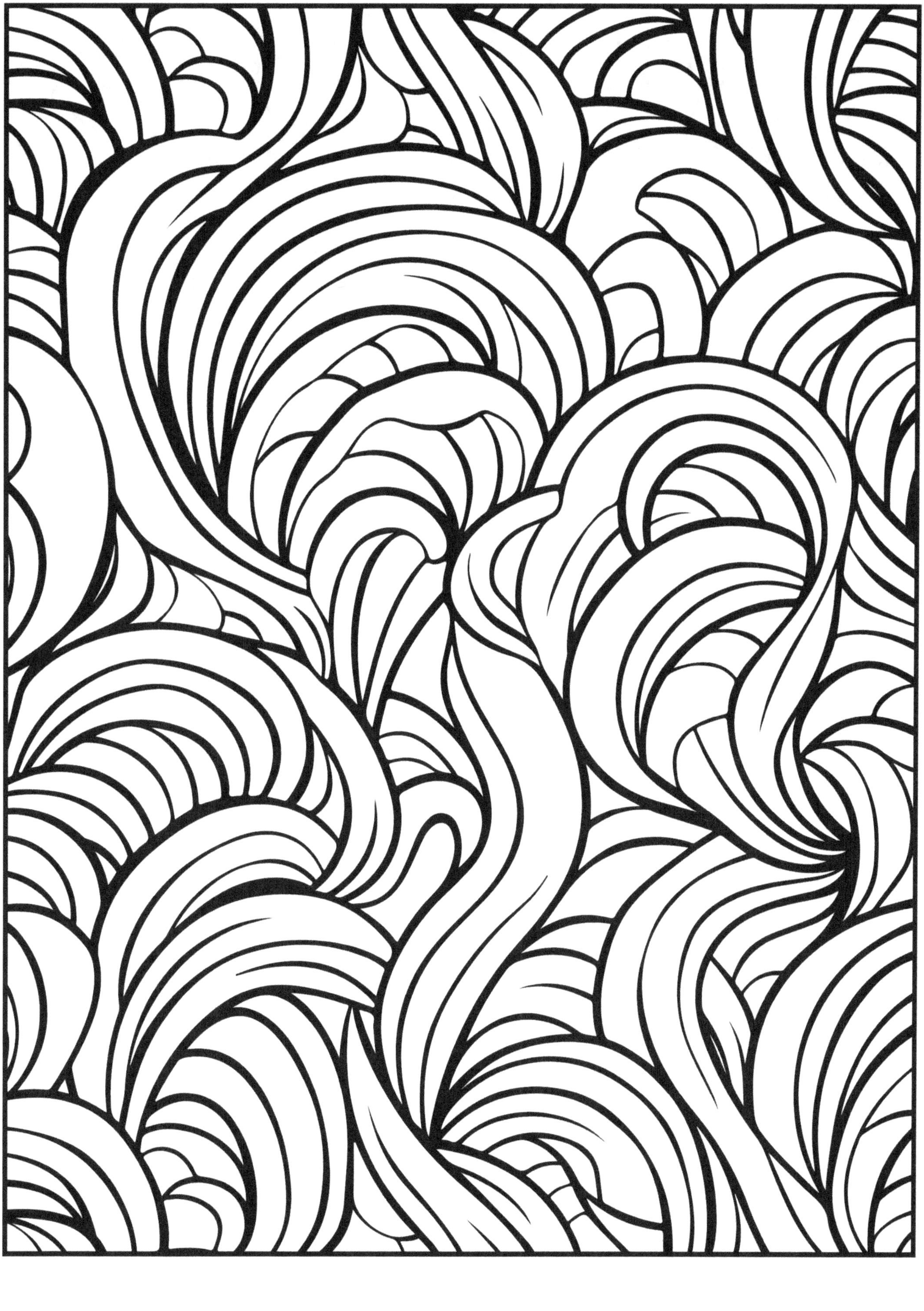

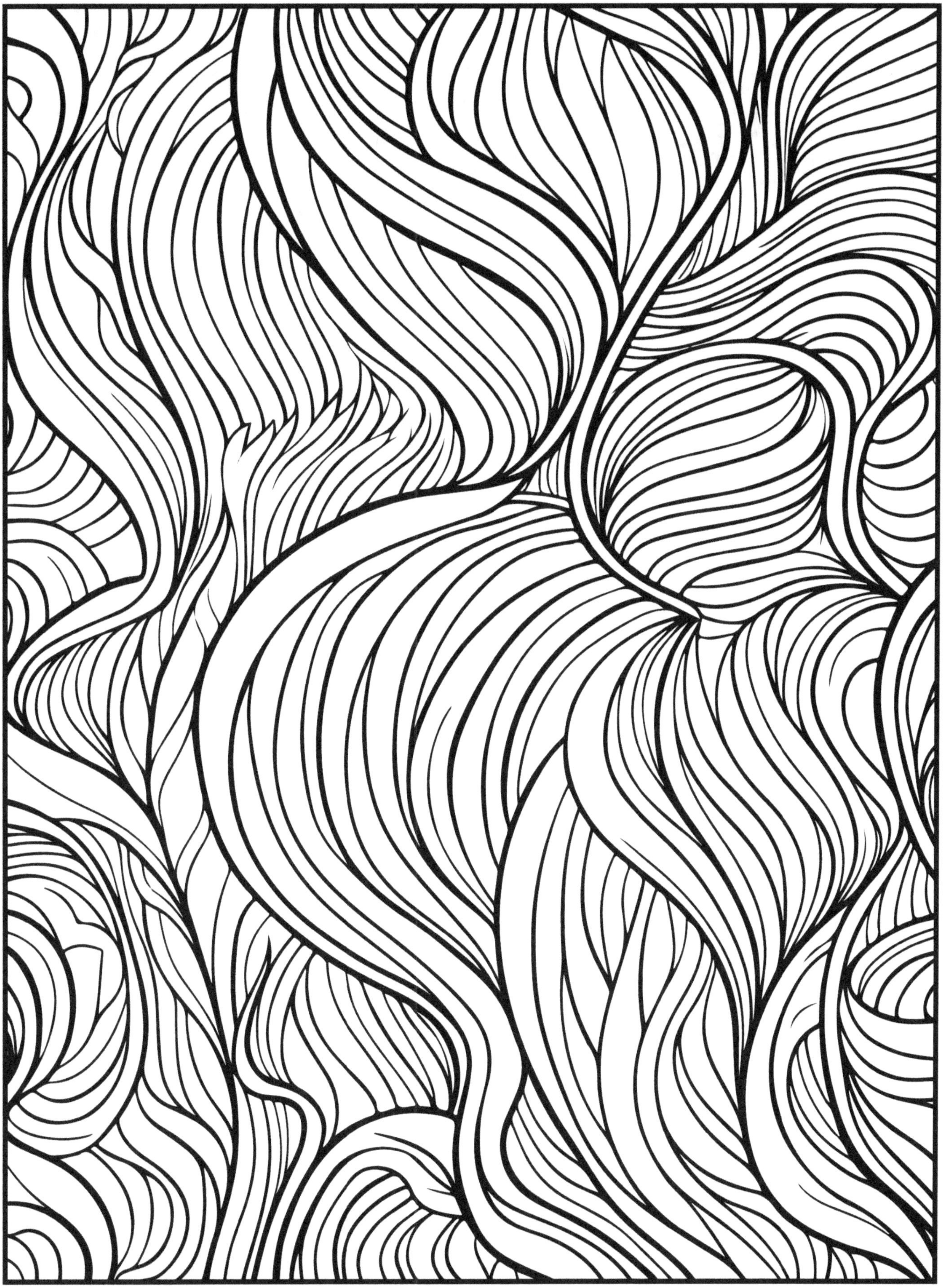

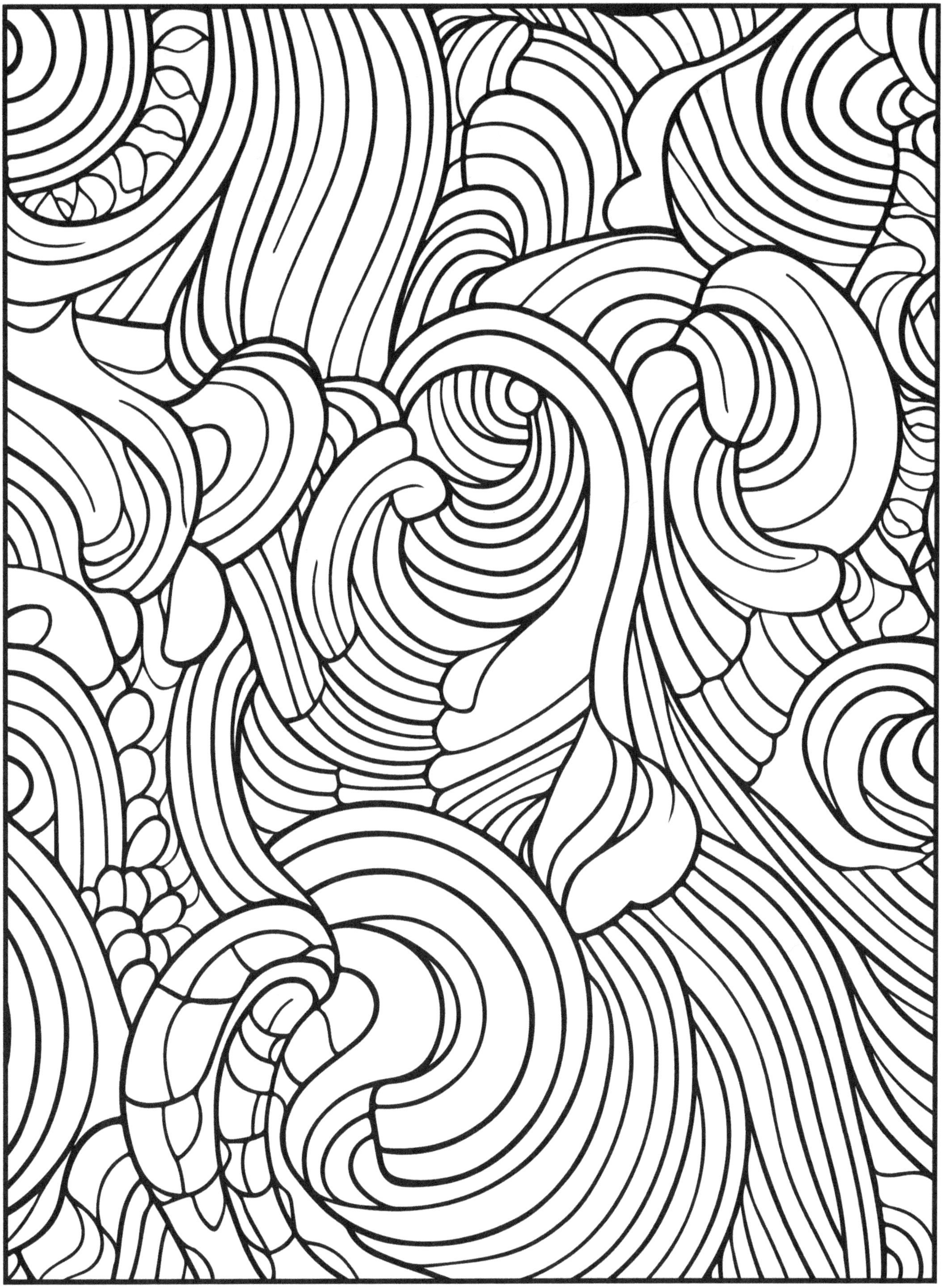

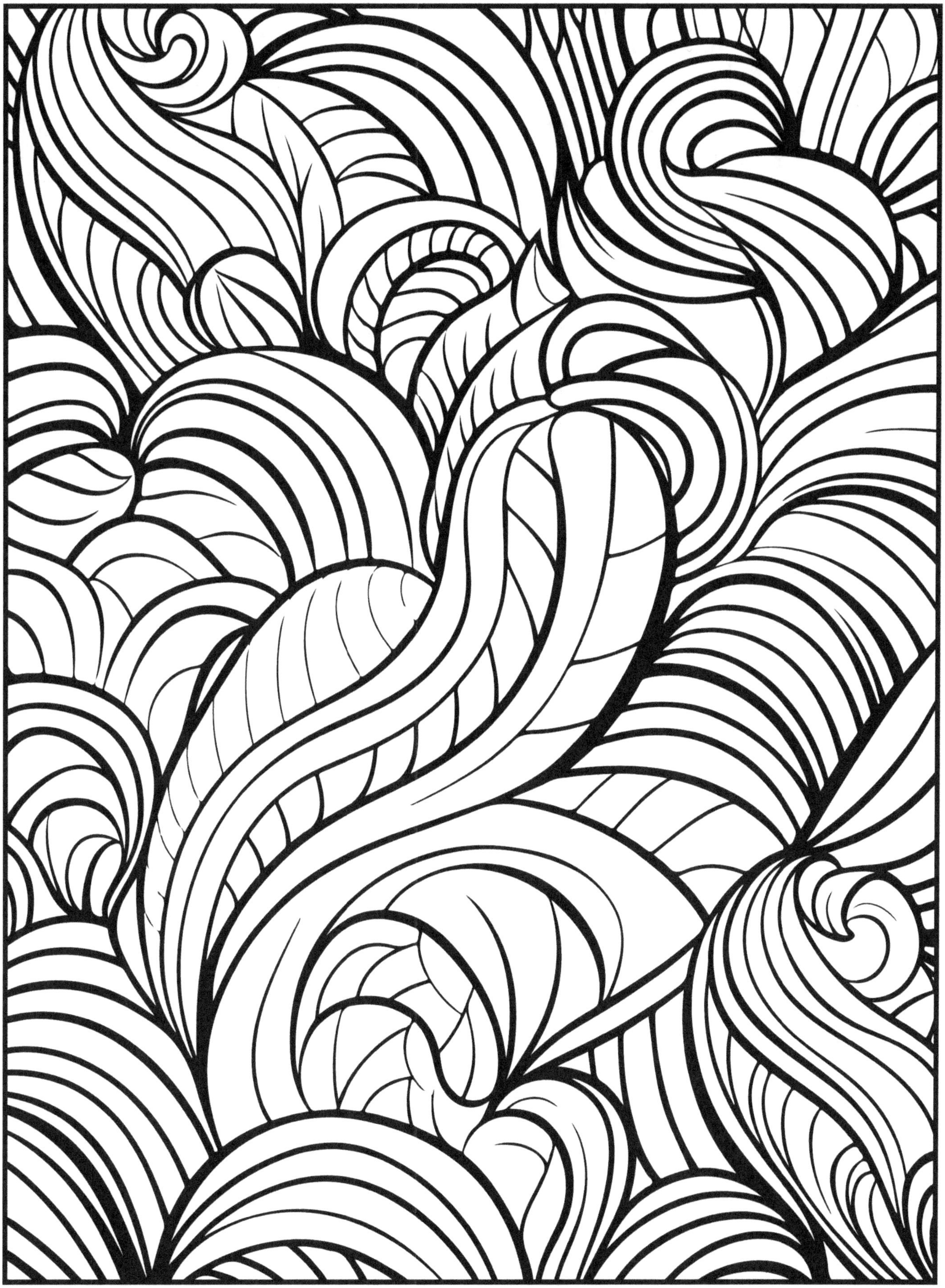

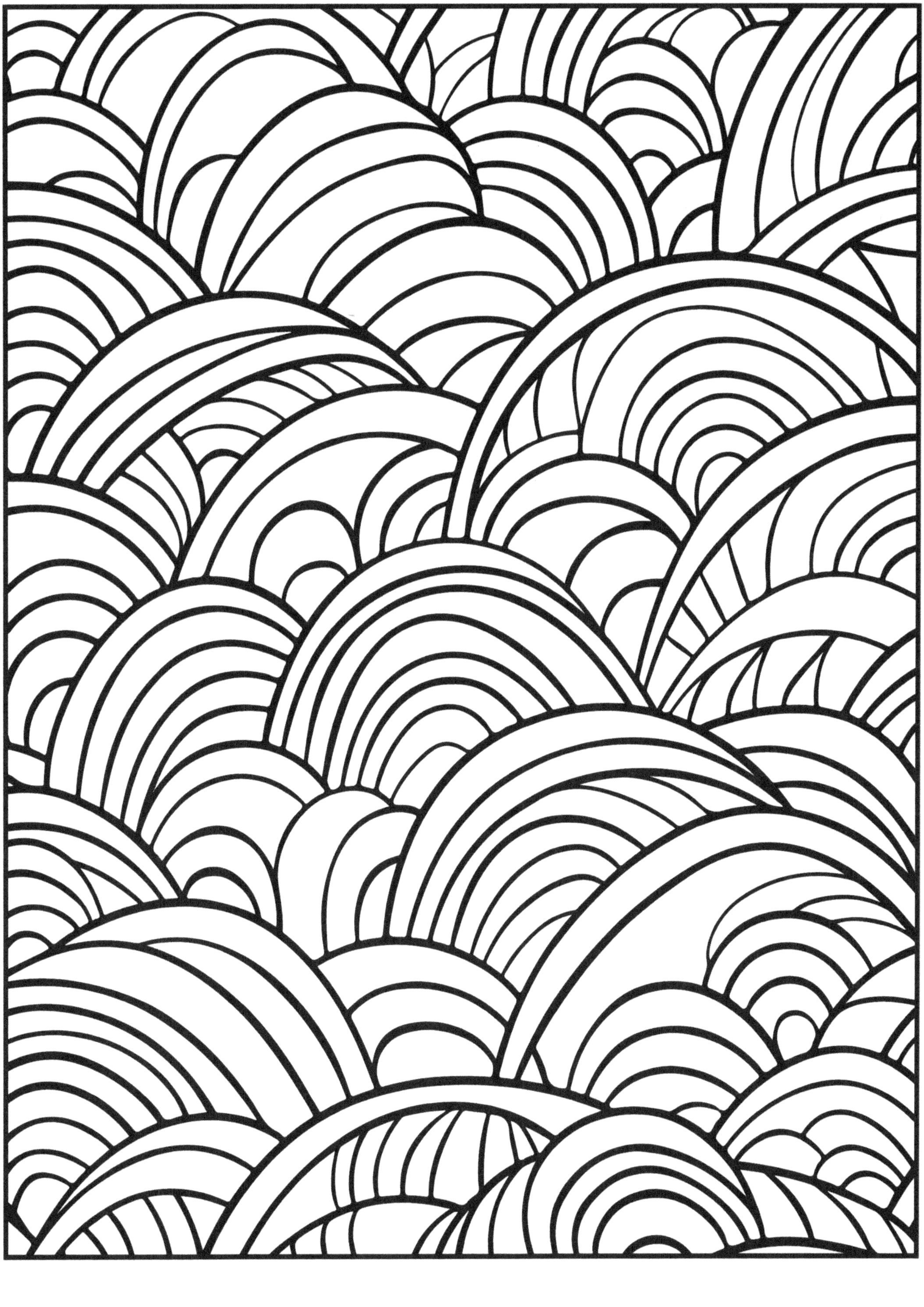

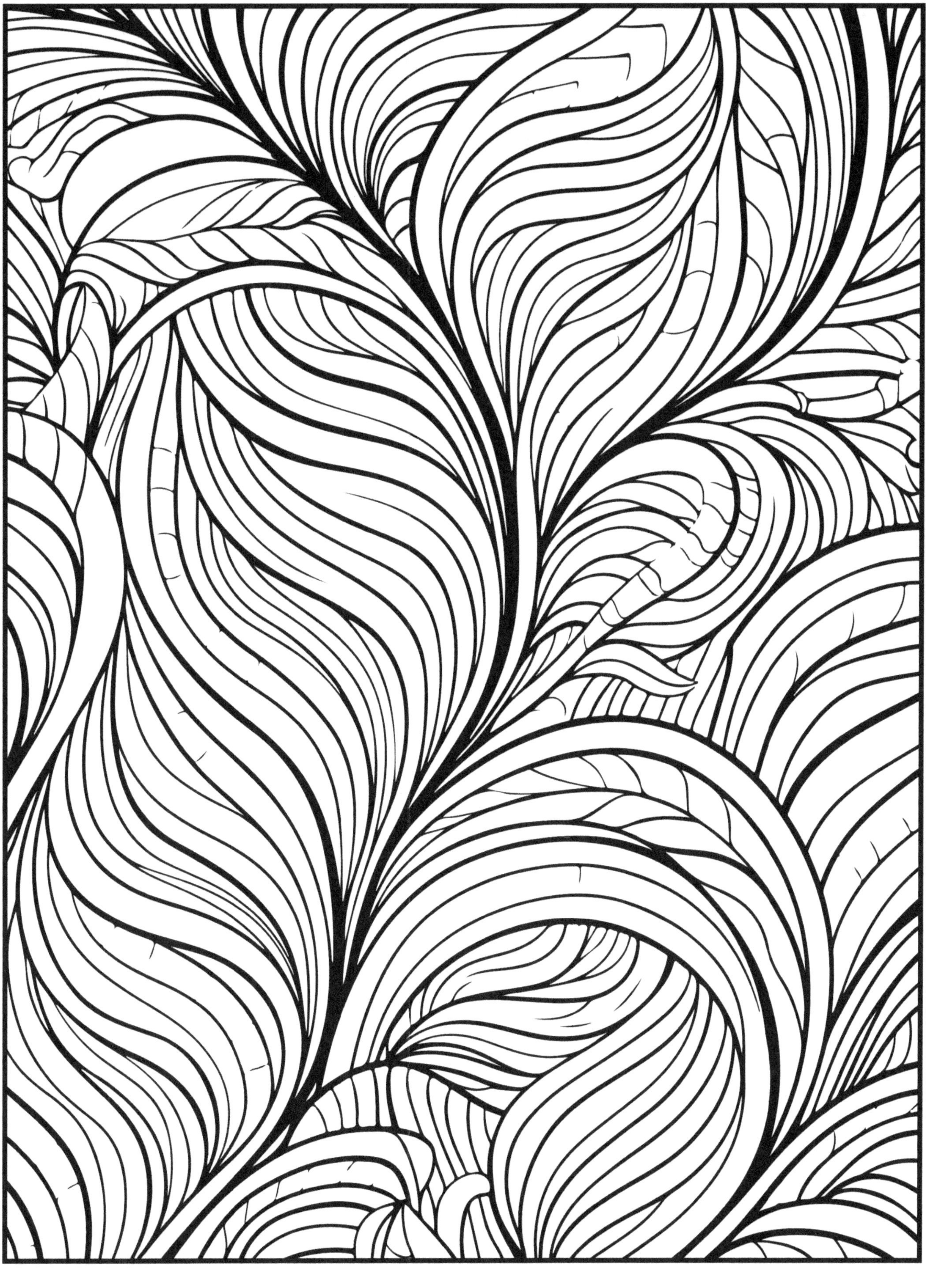

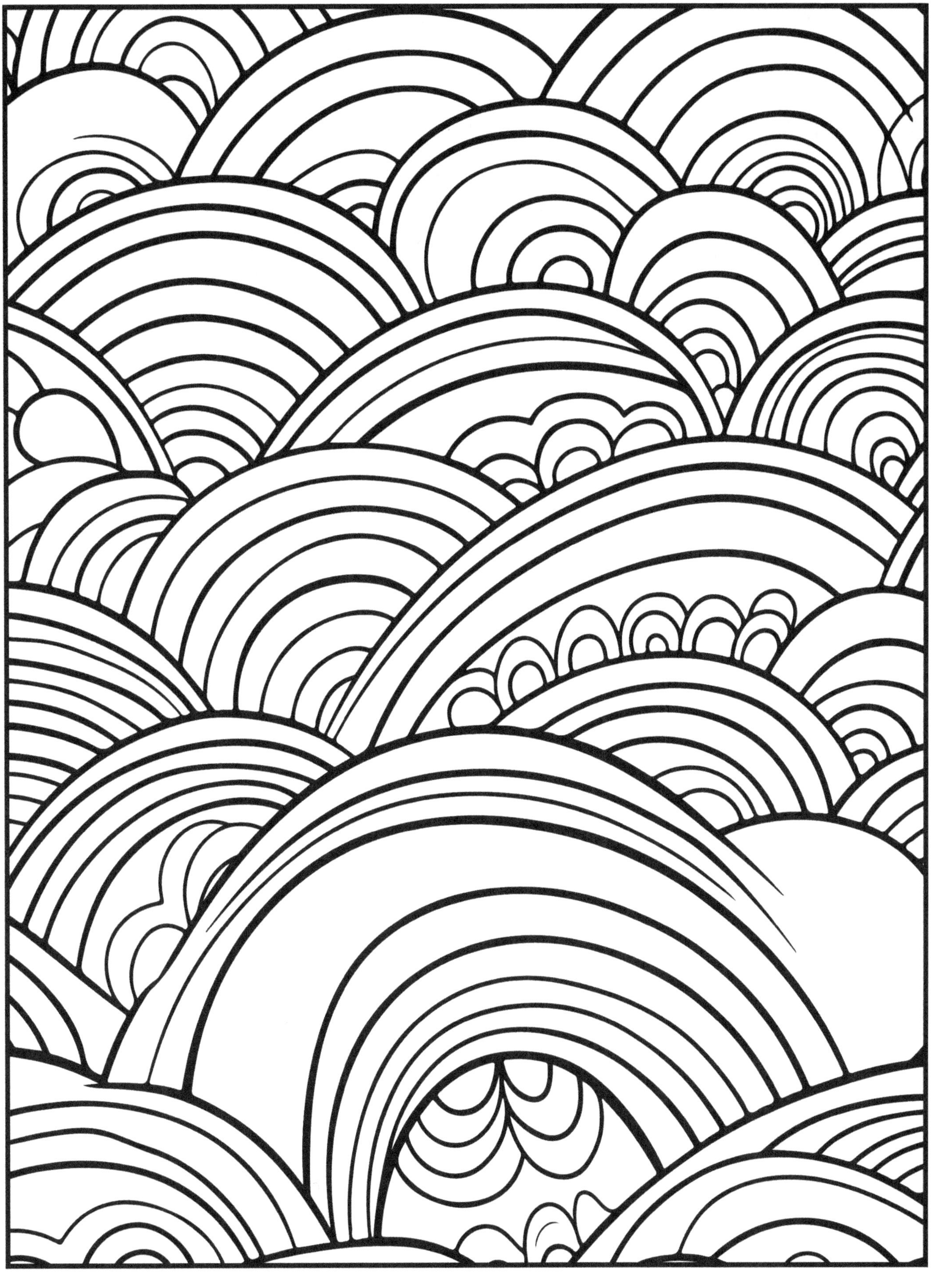

www.ingramcontent.com/pod-product-compliance
Lightning Source LLC
Chambersburg PA
CBHW082112220526
45472CB00009B/2148
* 9 7 9 8 3 2 7 7 5 8 3 8 4 *